W9-AGC-081

Presented to:

Brian Findley

Presented by:

Mom & Larry

Date:

12- 25-02

E-MAIL FROM GOD FOR MEN

by

Andy Cloninger

RIVER
OAK

PUBLISHING

Tulsa, Oklahoma

Unless otherwise indicated, all scripture quotations are taken from the *New American Standard Bible.* Copyright © The Lockman Foundation 1960, 1962, 1963, 1968, 1971, 1972, 1973, 1975, 1977, 1995. Used by permission.

E-mail from God for Men
ISBN 1-58919-999-5
Copyright © 2001 by Andy Cloninger
Represented by: Alive Communications, Inc.
7680 Goddard Street
Suite 200
Colorado Springs, CO 80920

Published by RiverOak Publishing
P.O. Box 700143
Tulsa, OK 74170-0143

Printed in the United States of America. All rights reserved under International Copyright Law. Contents and/or cover may not be reproduced in whole or in part in any form without the express written consent of the Publisher.

DEDICATION

This book is dedicated to my incredible wife, Jenni,
and to my wonderful children, Kaylee and Drew.
You have all inspired me to seek God's call to
true manhood and a deeper faith.

INTRODUCTION

Imagine that God Himself was really interested in you as a person. Imagine that He cared about your life, your family, your job, your hobbies, and even the secret desires and dreams of your heart. What would God say to you? And how would you respond?

Well, the truth is that God is crazy about you and is constantly reaching out, speaking to you. This book is written as if God found out your e-mail address (which would be very easy for Him to do) and began writing you personal e-mails. Each of these e-mails is based on Scripture and laced with a story, parable, or easy-to-understand message from the heart of God. No matter where you are in your relationship with God, you will find inspiration and meaning that you can apply to your life in a practical way.

God is calling forth a godly generation of men—men who are real about their faith and gut-level honest about their fears, struggles, and victories; men who are loving toward their families and friends and who are genuinely concerned about the needs of people around them. If you desire to be this kind of man, read on. Use these devotionals in your time with God, and hear what He wants to say to you today.

Andy Cloninger

THERE'S A BREAK IN THE CUP

We have this treasure in earthen vessels, so that the surpassing greatness of the power will be of God and not from ourselves.

2 Corinthians 4:7

My Son,

>When you first began to follow me, I filled you with my Spirit until you were overflowing with my love, peace, and joy. You felt as though you could walk on water and nothing could ever get you down again.

But you can't cruise forever on the salvation experience. You need daily filling, because you are a broken cup. Your brokenness allows my love to leak out, and you are left feeling empty all over again.

So come to me and live in my presence daily. Receive a fresh filling of my Spirit every morning. You'll never have to be empty again.

The Love That Overflows,
>God

== == ==   == == == == == == == == ==

A GIVING HEART

Remember the words of the Lord Jesus, that He Himself said, "It is more blessed to give than to receive."

Acts 20:35

My Child,

>I want you to experience the freedom that comes from giving your possessions and money for the work of my kingdom. Everything you have is mine already, whether you believe that or not. But if you live under the misconception that you are the owner of all I've put into your hands, you will have a hoarding heart. When you have a hoarding heart, you are fearful of loss and suspicious of others, so you become a slave to your possessions. You are never satisfied and always want more.

I have instituted giving as a way for you to overcome a hoarding heart. Do you really think I need your money? I already own everything. I want you to give so that you will be blessed. I'm not talking about the "give so you will receive lots of money" doctrine. I'm talking about being blessed with a heart of freedom that looks for ways to bless others and build up my kingdom. Be wise with what I've given you, and relinquish your ownership to me. Then you will be truly free.

Owner of Everything,
>God

== == ==   == == == == == == == == ==

A LAME SALES PITCH

These nations, which you are about to dispossess, give heed to soothsayers and to diviners; but as for you, the Lord your God has not allowed you so to do.

Deuteronomy · 18:14 RSV

My Son,

>There are many people making sales pitches for modern religions. They view Christianity as a dusty relic in an antique shop.

"Don't you know there are more streamlined and culturally relative beliefs available at Faith-Mart around the corner?" they say. "These faiths can put you more in control. In fact, why would you want to worship God when we could set it up for you to *be* God. After all, isn't your personal spirituality about making you feel good?"

The only problem with this sales pitch is that there is no redemption, no solid foundation, no absolute truth. It's like painting a watercolor portrait in the rain. It doesn't last. But following me is like sculpting the perfect you in marble. You are my treasure, my son. Don't buy into cheaper faiths.

Your Father,
>God

== == ==   == == == == == == == == ==

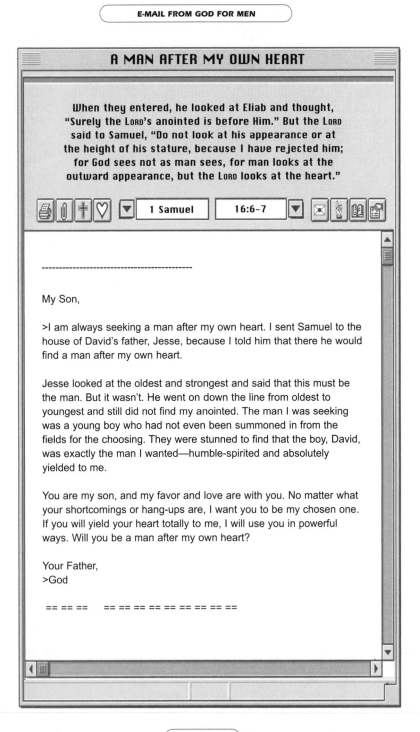

A MAN AFTER MY OWN HEART

When they entered, he looked at Eliab and thought, "Surely the Lord's anointed is before Him." But the Lord said to Samuel, "Do not look at his appearance or at the height of his stature, because I have rejected him; for God sees not as man sees, for man looks at the outward appearance, but the Lord looks at the heart."

| 1 Samuel | 16:6-7 |

My Son,

>I am always seeking a man after my own heart. I sent Samuel to the house of David's father, Jesse, because I told him that there he would find a man after my own heart.

Jesse looked at the oldest and strongest and said that this must be the man. But it wasn't. He went on down the line from oldest to youngest and still did not find my anointed. The man I was seeking was a young boy who had not even been summoned in from the fields for the choosing. They were stunned to find that the boy, David, was exactly the man I wanted—humble-spirited and absolutely yielded to me.

You are my son, and my favor and love are with you. No matter what your shortcomings or hang-ups are, I want you to be my chosen one. If you will yield your heart totally to me, I will use you in powerful ways. Will you be a man after my own heart?

Your Father,
>God

== == ==   == == == == == == == == ==

A THANKFUL HEART IS A HUMBLE HEART

**Give thanks in all circumstances;
for this is God's will for you in Christ Jesus.**

1 Thessalonians	5:18 NIV

My Son,

>The man who counts his sorrows is a prideful man because he always thinks someone owes him something more. But the man who counts his blessings is a humble man. He is overwhelmed with gratitude for what he was given but didn't deserve.

You are the only one who can choose which kind of man you're going to be. Everyone has sorrows in his life, and everyone has been given tremendous blessings. It's up to you to choose to have a heart of gratitude for the blessings I've showered down on you. Then you will experience the contentment that only a grateful heart can know. Count your blessings.

The Giver of All Good Things,
>God

== == ==   == == == == == == == == ==

A TRUTHFUL HEART

A lying tongue hates those it hurts,
and a flattering mouth works ruin.

Proverbs **26:28** NIV

My Child,

>What you say matters. It is so easy to fall into the trap of
exaggeration or flattery or flat-out lying. Though dishonesty can
sometimes get you what you want or help you avoid what you don't
want, steer clear of it. Though others may tell "little white lies" and get
away with them, I want you to be a man of absolute truth.

Why is honesty so important? It's not because I'm trying to make you
into a prideful goody-goody. It's because I want to develop you into a
man of character. I want you to experience the freedom that comes
from shooting straight. I want you to be delivered from the insecurity
that makes you exaggerate things to make yourself appear better
than you are.

Honesty is a matter of the heart. Give me your heart, and together
let's set honesty as our goal.

The Truth,
>God

== == ==   == == == == == == == == ==

ASK ME FOR WHAT YOU WANT

You do not have because you do not ask.

| James | 4:2 |

My Child,

>Ask me for what you want. If you need direction, ask me. If you need knowledge, I will give it to you. If you need the freedom to be creative, I am the most creative being in existence.

Don't be afraid to ask me for anything. Don't assume that I will laugh at you or put you off. Sometimes you don't have the things you need because you simply don't ask. Don't doubt my love for you. Because I love you, I will give you only things that will bless you.

I'm not necessarily talking about your asking me for a million dollars or a fancy luxury car. You don't even know whether those things would be blessings or curses in your life. I know what you need, and I will provide all of your needs. That's a promise.

Your Provider,
>God

== == ==   == == == == == == == == ==

BE STILL

Be still, and know that I am God; I will be exalted among the nations, I will be exalted in the earth.

Psalm | **46:10** NIV

My Son,

>Be still and know that I am God. Seek stillness and calmness as other men seek money or power.

People move at such a frantic speed. If something isn't ready in under a minute, they ask, "Why is it taking so long?" This busy existence is the killer of the spiritual man.

Instant gratification is the mantra of the modern world. Sadly, it is also becoming a mantra which is chanted in the church. Some people want a spiritual drive-up window attached to my house.

Stillness is the life of the spiritual man. Calmness is a countercultural lifestyle in the midst of all the motion. When you sit still and know my reality, I give you clarity to see the lie of the fast and furious. Come into my presence. Take time to know me, to hear me, and to become who I am calling you to be.

Your Peace,
>God

== == ==   == == == == == == == == ==

BRING IT TO THE TOMB

We were therefore buried with Him through
Baptism into death in order that, just as Christ
was raised from the dead through the glory
of the Father, we too may live a new life.

Romans   6:4 NIV

My Child,

>Whatever you take into the tomb and lay down next to Jesus is
dead. More than that, it is resurrected into a new identity and set in
order in the new you.

But whatever you refuse to take into the tomb and lay down with Jesus
has not died in you, and it continues to have a stake in your life.

If you want to be a totally new creation, bring everything to the tomb.
Bring it through prayer and repentance and lay it down next to Jesus.
Let the old man die with him through his sacrifice.

Then let him raise you to new life with him. Be totally redeemed in the
light of his resurrection. Bring everything to the tomb and then pass
through to new life.

Your Redeemer,
>God

== == ==   == == == == == == == == ==

COME HOME

So he got up and came to his father. But while he was still a long way off, his father saw him and felt compassion for him, and ran and embraced him and kissed him. . . . The father said to his slaves, "Quickly bring out the best robe and put it on him, and put a ring on his hand and sandals on his feet."

Luke 15:20,22

My Son,

>Whenever you come home to me, I don't make you beat the door down and beg to be a servant in my house. I run to meet you. I restore to you what you wasted. I throw a party in honor of your return.

Don't think that my love gives up on you when you choose to leave me. I am not a father who holds you at arm's length. Instead, I wait to have you close to me. I wait at the window, running shoes on, ready to rush out and welcome you home.

You will always be my son, no matter what choices you make. My love is the robe that covers you. My grace is the ring I place on your finger. My acceptance is like a pair of magical shoes on your feet that always brings you home to me. Never hesitate. Come home.

Your Father,
>God

== == ==   == == == == == == == == ==

CONVICTION IS NOT GUILT

There is therefore now no condemnation to them which are in Christ Jesus, who walk not after the flesh, but after the Spirit. For the law of the Spirit of life in Christ Jesus hath made me free from the law of sin and death.

Romans   8:1–2 KJV

My Child,

>There is a difference between the conviction that my Holy Spirit brings and the guilt that Satan brings or that you place on yourself. Conviction always leads you to repentance and makes you want to get right with me. It produces a positive result—a restored relationship with me. Guilt tells you, "You're no good. You can't ever be right with God." Guilt doesn't lead to repentance. It leads to moral dishonesty and low self-esteem, which lead away from me and into more guilt.

For those who are in my Son, Jesus Christ, there is always hope and a way out of the negative guilt cycle. When you sin, hear my Holy Spirit's call of true conviction. Repent honestly. Accept my forgiveness through Jesus, and allow him to move you onward and upward.

Your Forgiver,
>God

== == ==   == == == == == == == == ==

COUNT YOUR BLESSINGS AND MOVE ON

Not returning evil for evil or insult for insult, but giving a blessing instead; for you were called for the very purpose that you might inherit a blessing.

| 1 Peter | 3:9 |

My Child,

>Lots of men are disappointed in the way their parents raised them. Some of them live their whole lives trying to undo childhood wrongs. Others spend their entire lives harboring bitterness toward their parents.

I am calling you to be a new creation. If you're still struggling with things your parents did wrong in raising you, here's what I suggest. First, make a list of everything that your parents did right and be grateful for them. Then make a list of all the things your parents did wrong. Take this list of wrongs and surrender it to me in prayer, or pray about it with a friend or pastor. Then burn the "wrong" list, and choose to move on. Even if you feel as if you never inherited a blessing from your parents, when you forgive them, you will inherit my blessing of being free from resentment and bitterness. Don't let your past rule your present or your future. I am making you a new creation.

Your Hope for Healing,
>God

== == ==   == == == == == == == == ==

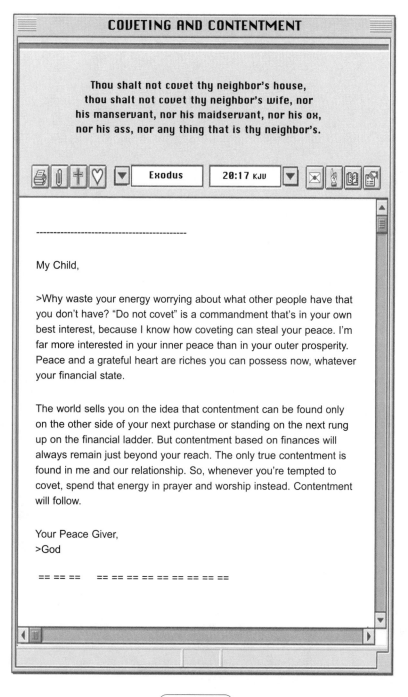

COVETING AND CONTENTMENT

Thou shalt not covet thy neighbor's house,
thou shalt not covet thy neighbor's wife, nor
his manservant, nor his maidservant, nor his ox,
nor his ass, nor any thing that is thy neighbor's.

Exodus 20:17 KJV

My Child,

>Why waste your energy worrying about what other people have that
you don't have? "Do not covet" is a commandment that's in your own
best interest, because I know how coveting can steal your peace. I'm
far more interested in your inner peace than in your outer prosperity.
Peace and a grateful heart are riches you can possess now, whatever
your financial state.

The world sells you on the idea that contentment can be found only
on the other side of your next purchase or standing on the next rung
up on the financial ladder. But contentment based on finances will
always remain just beyond your reach. The only true contentment is
found in me and our relationship. So, whenever you're tempted to
covet, spend that energy in prayer and worship instead. Contentment
will follow.

Your Peace Giver,
>God

== == ==   == == == == == == == == ==

DON'T BE AFRAID TO DECIDE

Deal courageously, and may the LORD be with the upright!

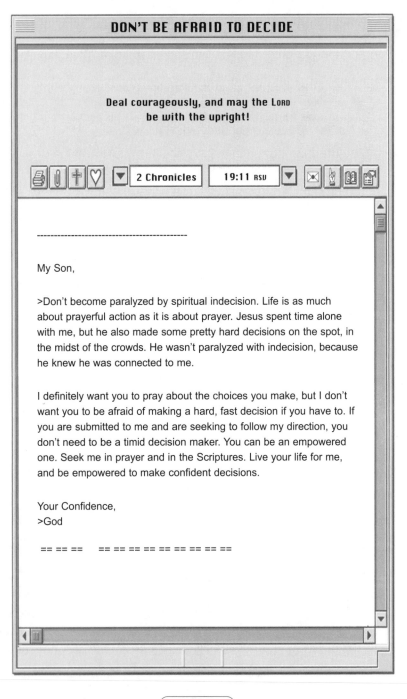

2 Chronicles 19:11 RSV

My Son,

>Don't become paralyzed by spiritual indecision. Life is as much about prayerful action as it is about prayer. Jesus spent time alone with me, but he also made some pretty hard decisions on the spot, in the midst of the crowds. He wasn't paralyzed with indecision, because he knew he was connected to me.

I definitely want you to pray about the choices you make, but I don't want you to be afraid of making a hard, fast decision if you have to. If you are submitted to me and are seeking to follow my direction, you don't need to be a timid decision maker. You can be an empowered one. Seek me in prayer and in the Scriptures. Live your life for me, and be empowered to make confident decisions.

Your Confidence,
>God

== == ==   == == == == == == == == ==

DON'T CRITICIZE THE CREATION

Will the clay say to the potter, "What are you doing?"
Or the thing you are making say, "He has no hands"?
Woe to him who says to a father, "What are you begetting?"
Or to a woman, "To what are you giving birth?"

| Isaiah | 45:9-10 |

My Son,

>You are my perfect creation. I am totally pleased with you. It hurts me when you aren't pleased with yourself. If you are critical of the way you are made, then you are being critical of me, the Maker.

If you built a beautiful piece of furniture for your best friend and all that friend did was take it home and complain about the color and the shape, it would hurt your feelings. That's how I feel when you cut yourself down.

You are wonderful to me. That's how I see you, and that's how I want you to see yourself.

Your Builder,
>God

== == ==   == == == == == == == == ==

DON'T HOLD IT ABOVE THE WATER

A certain man named Ananias, with Sapphira his wife, sold a possession, and kept back part of the price, his wife also being privy to it, and brought a certain part, and laid it at the apostles' feet.

Acts   5:1-2 KJV

My Child,

>During the Crusades of the twelfth century, some crusaders hired mercenary warriors to fight in their place. Because it was a war being fought for "religious" reasons, the crusaders required the mercenaries to be baptized before going off to fight.

As they were being baptized, the mercenaries let themselves go under the water, but they held their swords above the water because they didn't want to submit the use of their swords to Jesus.

What is it that you are holding out of the water right now in your Christian walk? What is it that you feel you can do a better job of controlling than I can? There's nothing to fear, because you know that I have your best interests in mind. I want to bring those high and dry areas of your life under the water of baptism and use them to bless you and not to harm you.

Your Father,
>God

== == ==   == == == == == == == == ==

DON'T LOSE THE WONDER

**Why did I come forth from the womb to see
toil and sorrow, and spend my days in shame?**

| Jeremiah | 20:18 RSV |

My Son,

>Don't lose your awareness of the mystery of life or the beauty of
being alive. I know that it can be so tempting to just fall into the rut of
checking things off your daily list and going to bed, only to wake up
the next day and start all over. There is more to life than that!

I have placed beautiful things in the world for you to see on your way
to work. Open your eyes to see them. I have given you moments in
every day to notice the goodness that is still in humanity. Notice them.
Most importantly, I have given you a will to choose the wonder of daily
living over the despair of daily dying. Choose the wonder. If you have
fallen asleep to what's all around you, it's time to let me wake you up
to this celebration called life.

Creator of All Life,
>God

== == ==   == == == == == == == == ==

DON'T TRY TO GO BACK

I press on toward the goal for the prize of the upward call of God in Christ Jesus.

Philippians 3:14

My Child,

>I know it's tempting to look back at a mountaintop time in your spiritual journey and think, *I just need to get back to that place.* But the spiritual journey is not about getting back to any place, no matter how good that place was. It is about moving forward towards the goal.

Today is the best place you've ever been, regardless of the current circumstances. That's because today is full of miraculous possibilities. I have brought you to this point in time for a purpose, and I am leading you on to achieve the goals I have for you.

If you're not in a "good" place right now, don't be tempted to reminisce about more spiritual times in your life. Thank me for the sanctity and awesomeness of this place and time. I love you just as much today as I did on that mountaintop. Don't spend your energy trying to get back there. Start exactly where you are, and let's move on to even more amazing places together.

The Guide on Your Journey,
>God

== == ==   == == == == == == == == ==

FASTING AGAINST THE FLESH

**Go, gather all the Jews to be found in Susa,
and hold a fast on my behalf, and neither
eat nor drink for three days, night or day.**

| | Esther | 4:16 RSV | |

My Child,

>A lot of people misunderstand the power of fasting and prayer. They think that fasting is a way to show how serious and holy they are, but that's not the point.

Fasting is a great way for your spiritual man to tell your fleshly, or carnal, man to take the backseat. If you're always giving your flesh what it wants, you're placing it in the driver's seat. At that point, it's no wonder that it steers you wherever it wants you to go. But if you deny your flesh on a regular basis, your spirit can be focused and in control.

If you're having trouble conquering temptation, fasting is a great way to master the flesh. It doesn't mean that you're more holy than someone who doesn't fast. It means that you're willing to ask for help in the battle over your own flesh. Submit to me, and I'll help you in the battle.

Your Strength,
>God

== == ==   == == == == == == == == ==

GREAT EXPECTATIONS

May the God of hope fill you with all joy and
peace in believing, so that by the power of
the Holy Spirit you may abound in hope.

| Romans | 15:13 RSV |

My Son,

>Expect me to work wonderful things in your life. I will. Even if you
doubt that you are worth it, expect my merciful touch and my
transforming grace.

Because you are my son, I have plans to develop you into a top-
notch person. And because I love you so much, I get a kick out of
going beyond good in your life and increasing it to great. Even earthly
fathers who love their sons want to give them the good things. How
much more do I want you to have joy in the life I've given you!

Now that you're mine, you are going to have a growing, expanding
life; a greater and deeper group of friends; an ever-broadening set of
experiences and gifts. You are an heir to my kingdom. Don't sell
yourself short. Let's grow your life together.

The Lord of Great Expectations,
>God

== == ==   == == == == == == == == ==

HAND IN GLOVE

So God created man in his own image, in the image of God he created him; male and female he created them.

Genesis 1:27 NIV

My Child,

>I created you in my image. In the same way that a glove was created in the shape of a hand, I have made you into my shape.

Without a hand to fill it, a glove isn't fulfilling its purpose. But with a hand filling the glove, that glove can accomplish amazing things. The same is true of your relationship with me. I made you to be filled with my presence and my purpose for your life. You aren't shaped to be filled by anything else. That's why other things will never fill you completely. You were made for me.

Let me fill you, son. Let me show you the wonderful works I have created for you. Let me fulfill the purpose for which you were created.

Your Indweller,
>God

== == ==   == == == == == == == == ==

HAPPINESS VS. CONTENTMENT

I know how to get along with humble means, and I also know
how to live in prosperity; in any and every circumstance I
have learned the secret of being filled and going hungry,
both of having abundance and suffering need.

Philippians	4:12

My Son,

>Is your contentment based on your circumstances? Or is your
contentment based on your absolute surrender to my will in your life?

Contentment is not simply being happy with how things are going. It is
a deep, immovable peace that you can only experience once you've
placed your life totally in my hands. It is the serenity that can't be
moved by changes in circumstances or finances. Happiness can be
manufactured by favorable conditions, but contentment can't be
bought at any earthly price.

Son, I want you to stop trying to substitute happiness for contentment.
Happiness is a sugar cube that melts in your mouth; it's there one
minute and gone the next. Contentment is something not based on
taste, sight, or smell. It is knowing you'll never hunger again. Find that
contentment in me.

Your Father,
>God

== == ==   == == == == == == == == ==

HAVE MY HEART OF MERCY

Blessed are the merciful, for they will be shown mercy.

Matthew 5:7 NIV

My Child,

>The world is filled with people who tend to take a "guilty until proven innocent" attitude toward their fellow man. I don't want you to be this type of unforgiving person. Instead, pray for a heart that gives others the benefit of the doubt.

It's not wise to be down on someone else for messing up, because it may be only a matter of time until you're the one messing up and needing mercy. Jesus knew that everybody was capable of making mistakes, but he also knew that everybody was worth forgiving.

My son, choose to have the same merciful heart that Jesus had. Keep in mind all that he's forgiven in you. Let that humble and soften your heart toward those who let you down. You have been, and will always be, shown mercy.

Your Forgiver,
>God

== == ==   == == == == == == == == ==

HERE TODAY

**Do not ignore this one fact, beloved, that
with the Lord one day is as a thousand years,
and a thousand years as one day.**

| 2 Peter | 3:8 |

My Son,

>I'm not stuck in the B. C. period. I am not walking around every day in a terry cloth bath towel like the shepherds in your church's Christmas pageant. That era of time in the Bible is important, or I would never have bothered to write it down. But I'm not stuck there.

I am the God of yesterday, today, and forever. I am not only on the cutting edge of what's happening right now; I also know all the possibilities of what is to come.

So don't think of me as some old man who gets scared of riding fast in a modern car. You need to see me in your world today. I know everything that you're going through, and I'm right here with you in the present moment. Know me as I was and am and will be.

The Ultra Postmodern, Modern, and Futuristic,
>God

== == ==   == == == == == == == == ==

HIDE YOURSELF IN ME

The LORD is my rock, and my fortress, and my deliverer, my God, my rock, in whom I take refuge, my shield, and the horn of my salvation, my stronghold.

| Psalm | 18:2 RSV |

My Child,

>The words to a favorite hymn are "Rock of Ages, cleft for me, let me hide myself in thee." I am the unbreakable God who allowed himself to be broken upon the cross. In that breaking, a doorway was opened into the depth of my love and protection.

When you step through that opening, you are safe from any storm of life that would blow up around you. And when the sun shines hot in the desert times, you will stay covered and cool in my shadow.

I was broken for you so that you could find refuge in me. Step through the door of deliverance into the rock that was broken for you. Hide yourself in me.

Your Rock,
>God

== == ==   == == == == == == == == ==

I AM ALWAYS THERE

Who shall separate us from the love of Christ?

| Romans | 8:35 NIV |

My Child,

>Don't feel guilty if you haven't spent time with me in a while. I haven't given up on you. I do miss you, but it's still wonderful when we get together. If you let guilt build up about not spending time with me, it will actually keep you from meeting with me. You are mine, and nothing can truly separate us. Even if you feel that we're far apart, you're wrong. I am right here with you.

My desire for our relationship is that you would be fully mine, just as I'm already fully yours. I want more than our quiet times together. I like the quiet times, but I also like the noisy times and all the times in between. Open up your mind and your heart to me wherever you are, and I'll be there. Don't let guilt keep you from me.

Your Ever-present Father,
>God

== == ==   == == == == == == == == ==

I AM . . .

**God said to Moses, "I AM WHO I AM";
and He said, "Thus you shall say to the
sons of Israel, 'I AM has sent me to you.'"**

Exodus 3:14

My Child,

>Do you feel that you've really messed things up? I am the God of
forgiveness. Turn to me and receive it. Do you feel as if you just can't
make it through? I am the God of strength. Turn to me if you are
weary and heavy-laden, and I will give you my strength. Do you feel
as if you are so wound up that you don't have any peace? I am
peace. Turn to me and receive the peace you need. Do you feel
you've lost something along the way (your youth, your hope, your
innocence)? I am the God of restoration. Turn to me, and I will restore
what the world has stolen from you.

Because of who I am, you can be all you were meant to be. Because
of my Son's sacrifice, I can be with you in your suffering. Because of
his resurrection, I can give you power over all the worries that try to
steal your hope. I am all these things for you. Stay close to me.

I Am,
>God

== == ==   == == == == == == == == ==

I WILL ALWAYS GIVE YOU A WAY OUT

God is faithful; He will not let you be tempted beyond what you can bear. But when you are tempted, He will also provide a way out so that you can stand up under it.

1 Corinthians · 10:13 NIV

My Son,

>The biblical hero Joseph was enslaved to an Egyptian named Potipher. When Potipher's wife tried to entice Joseph to sleep with her, Joseph fled the room as if he were fleeing from death itself. He knew that to give in to that temptation would be to sin against me, and to him, that was worse than death. I provided a way out for him, but he had to run toward my provision and away from the world's temptation.

When you're in the jaws of temptation, I will always give you a way out. I will never allow you to be tempted beyond your strength, and I will give you conviction about what is right and wrong. But you are the one who has to act on those convictions and race toward my escape hatch.

So when you're in the grip of temptation, immediately begin looking for the escape I will provide. Be convinced that there will be a way out of every hard situation. Develop a keen eye and swift feet, and make tracks!

Your Escape from Sin,
>God

== == ==   == == == == == == == == ==

I WILL MEET WITH YOU

**Where two or three have gathered together
in My name, I am there in their midst.**

Matthew | 18:20

My Son,

>If you show up to worship me, expect me to meet you. Whenever two or more are gathered in my name, I am right in the middle of them.

If you showed up at the theater with tickets to see your favorite singer, you wouldn't sit there wondering if you were going to get to hear music that night. That's the way it's set up. You show up and cheer your lungs out; they show up and play their hearts out.

Worship is set up in a certain way as well. If you show up, I show up. It's our meeting time. Come to actively participate. Sing, cheer, pray, praise. Be excited. Seek my face. Listen for my voice. Jesus laid his heart out for you on the cross, and he continues to lay it out for you every day. Come with confidence when you worship. Jesus will meet you. So will I. And you'll have the time of your life!

See you there,
>God

== == ==   == == == == == == == == ==

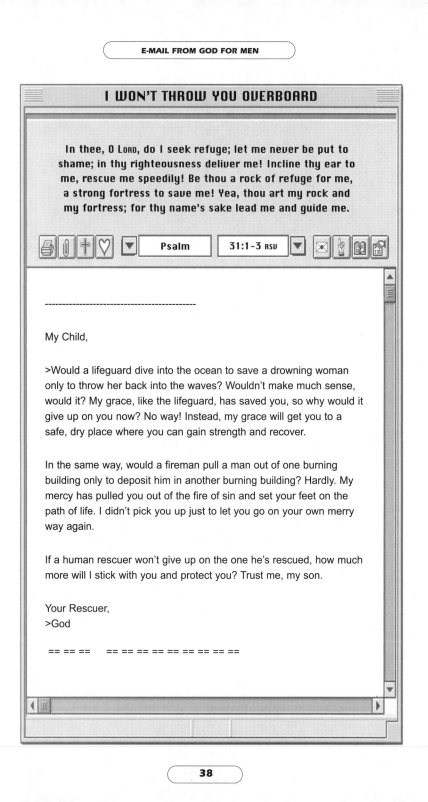

I WON'T THROW YOU OVERBOARD

In thee, O Lord, do I seek refuge; let me never be put to shame; in thy righteousness deliver me! Incline thy ear to me, rescue me speedily! Be thou a rock of refuge for me, a strong fortress to save me! Yea, thou art my rock and my fortress; for thy name's sake lead me and guide me.

Psalm 31:1-3 RSV

My Child,

>Would a lifeguard dive into the ocean to save a drowning woman only to throw her back into the waves? Wouldn't make much sense, would it? My grace, like the lifeguard, has saved you, so why would it give up on you now? No way! Instead, my grace will get you to a safe, dry place where you can gain strength and recover.

In the same way, would a fireman pull a man out of one burning building only to deposit him in another burning building? Hardly. My mercy has pulled you out of the fire of sin and set your feet on the path of life. I didn't pick you up just to let you go on your own merry way again.

If a human rescuer won't give up on the one he's rescued, how much more will I stick with you and protect you? Trust me, my son.

Your Rescuer,
>God

== == ==   == == == == == == == == ==

I DO NOT TEMPT YOU

Let no man say when he is tempted, I am tempted of God: for God cannot be tempted with evil, neither tempteth he any man: But every man is tempted, when he is drawn away of his own lust, and enticed. Then when lust hath conceived, it bringeth forth sin: and sin, when it is finished, bringeth forth death. Do not err, my beloved brethren.

James 1:13-16 KJV

My Child,

>I'm not out to tempt you or to trap you. I don't construct a spiritual obstacle course just to sit back and see how you do. I am working good things in your life so that you will be brought into my kingdom whole and complete.

I will never lead you into sin. Satan is the one who tempts men and tries to lead them into sin. He uses the same enticing lie he did in Eden. The lie is the promise that man can be like God. Man himself is to blame for believing that lie. It's the one that gets him into all his trouble.

So be on the lookout for temptation, my son, and call on the name of Jesus to deliver you from the real tempter.

The Victorious One,
>God

== == ==   == == == == == == == == ==

JOIN ME

One called out to another and said, "Holy, Holy, Holy, is the Lord of hosts, the whole earth is full of His glory."

| Isaiah | 6:3 |

My Child,

>I am working in the lives of everyone around you. I am in every place before you show up. I am loving every person before you even get a chance to love him or her.

Don't think that you are bringing my presence with you into any situation. I'm already there. Don't think that you are bringing me to someone I haven't already been seeking every day, calling his heart to me.

I want you to cooperate with me in accomplishing my purposes, but it is important for you to have the right perspective. Before you take the attitude that "I am Jesus to this person in this situation," ask instead, "How can I join the work that Jesus is already doing here?" I will surely use you.

Join me,
>God

== == ==   == == == == == == == == ==

KNOW ME WITH YOUR SPIRITUAL SENSES AS WELL

I pray that the eyes of your heart may be enlightened, so that you will know what is the hope of His calling, what are the riches of the glory of His inheritance in the saints.

Ephesians   **1:18**

My Son,

>You cannot know me with your physical mind alone. If you are seeking to understand me, you must use your spiritual faculties to perceive me correctly.

If you want to see me, you must use your spiritual eyes of faith to see what your physical eyes can't see. Open your spiritual eyes. If you want to hear me, you must use your spiritual ears of discernment to know what I'm saying to you. Hear my loving voice speaking to you. If you want to touch me, you must use your heart to reach out. I am not in this world now, but your heart can feel the touch of my Holy Spirit, who is present with you right now. Feel the touch of my hand. If you want to taste my goodness, you need to have a spiritual perspective of gratitude towards life. To the spiritual taster, life is good. Taste my goodness.

Let me awaken your spiritual senses, my child, so that you will know me fully.

Your Father,
>God

== == ==   == == == == == == == == ==

LAY IT ALL DOWN

Jesus answered them, saying, "The hour has come for the Son of Man to be glorified. Truly, truly, I say to you, unless a grain of wheat falls into the earth and dies, it remains alone; but if it dies, it bears much fruit. He who loves his life loses it, and he who hates his life in this world will keep it to life eternal."

John   12:23-25

My Child,

>Unless you are willing to lay down everything that's important to you, you will never bear fruit. Unless you offer up your whole life to me, you exist only for yourself, and you are spiritually useless.

But once you lay down your life in my hands, I can take that fertile hope of your life and make it bloom and then reproduce itself for my glory. A life totally yielded to me will be used to reach out and touch other lives and draw them supernaturally to me.

Once you've laid everything down, the morgue of self-surrender becomes the garden of life. It is life not only for you but for the people I will send you to. Lay everything down, my son, and watch what I can do with a surrendered heart.

Your Freedom,
>God

== == ==   == == == == == == == == ==

LEAVE THE RESULTS TO ME

**My God shall supply all your needs
according to his riches in glory by Christ Jesus.**

Philippians | 4:19 KJV

My Son,

>Suppose the most acclaimed pastry chef in the world gave you his world-famous recipe for your wife's favorite cake so you could bake it for her birthday. The chef bought all the ingredients, laid them out in order, and explained the recipe. If you followed the directions perfectly, you wouldn't have to worry about the results.

If you are doing the best you can to follow my will, then you can leave the results to me. I have given you my word of instruction. I've laid out your plan to salvation and the abundant life. You don't have to sit around and fret about what your life will look like when it comes "out of the oven." It's going to be a culinary masterpiece.

Son, don't worry about the end results. Just follow me with your whole heart.

The Master Chef,
>God

== == ==   == == == == == == == == ==

LET THE RIVER FLOW THROUGH YOU

Each will be like a hiding place from the wind, a covert from the tempest, like streams of water in a dry place, like the shade of a great rock in a weary land.

| | Isaiah | 32:2 RSV | | |

My Son,

>There's something you've got to know about my love. It's not just given to you for your own warm fuzzy spiritual feeling. If you don't share it with others, it dries up.

My love was meant to be a river, flowing through you and out into the world. If you try to dam it up and make it into your own personal lake, it will evaporate from your life and you'll be left wondering why it left. You'll say, "But I'm praying, I'm worshipping, I'm spending my quiet time with God." But are you loving? Are you sharing my love with the world? Are you laying down your life for others?

If you're reaching out to others, if you're loving as a servant, you are widening the riverbanks and allowing my waters of life to flow as they were meant to. So don't dam the river. Let it flow.

The River of Life,
>God

== == ==   == == == == == == == == ==

LET'S RIDE

**Thy promise is well tried, and
your servant loves it.**

Psalm 119:140 RSV

My Son,

>Many people spend their energy avoiding challenges. These are the people who think they've got a great job if it pays them well and they don't really have to do anything.

Son, don't buy into this lie. The best jobs are the ones that challenge you to do more than you ever thought you could. They leave you amazed at your own abilities. Challenging work like this leaves you more fulfilled than you ever imagined you could be.

I have placed so many gifts and abilities in you. It's as though you are a high-performance race car built to run in top gear. So don't cruise in the slow lane. Don't be afraid of the challenge. Let's ride.

Your Driver,
>God

== == ==   == == == == == == == == ==

LIMITLESS PROVISION

They said to Him, "We have here only five loaves and two fish." And He said, "Bring them here to Me." . . . He blessed the food, and breaking the loaves He gave them to the disciples, and the disciples gave them to the crowds, and they all ate and were satisfied.

Matthew | 14:17-20

My Son,

>I am able to do so much more than you can imagine with what you offer me. Little becomes a lot when it's in my hands. Remember how Jesus fed the crowd of five thousand people? They looked at what they had from a human perspective and saw a few fish and some bread, but Jesus looked with eyes of faith and saw the perfect meal for five thousand people. You need to begin to see your "limitations" from my perspective. There are no barriers to how and what I can provide for you.

Trust in my abilities to meet your every need. If you have limited resources, bring them to me. Place them in my hands. I will bless them and make them more. And then, be prepared to eat and be satisfied.

Your Limitless Provider,
>God

== == ==   == == == == == == == == ==

LISTEN

Know this, my beloved brethren. Let every man be quick to hear, slow to speak, slow to anger.

James | 1:19 RSV

My Son,

>What kind of person would you go to if you needed to talk—if you needed someone to simply listen and not judge you? You would go to a trusted and caring friend. This isn't true only for you; it's true for the people in your life. Where does your wife go when she needs to talk and be heard? Where do your children go? Where do your friends go? Are you the friend that they can trust to take the time and really listen?

Most men are known for their impatience and quick-fix advice. I am calling you to be a different kind of man: quick to listen, slow to speak, not needing to fix problems in such a hurry. If you don't know how to be this kind of man, I will teach you. I want the people around you to be able to say of you at the end of your life, "He was someone I could always go to and talk with about anything. He was really there for me. I never had to go through anything alone because of him." Let me make you into that kind of friend.

The Friend Who's Always Here for You,
>God

== == ==   == == == == == == == == ==

LOVE ME BY LOVING YOUR BROTHER

If someone says, "I love God," and hates his brother, he is
a liar; for the one who does not love his brother whom
he has seen, cannot love God whom he has not seen.
And this commandment we have from Him, that
the one who loves God should love his brother also.

| | 1 John | | 4:20-21 | | |

My Son,

>Since you love me, I want you to love the people and the things that I love. If you want to know whom I love, look at the people Jesus loved when he was on earth. He loved tax collectors and outcasts. He also loved priests and those in power. He loved Jews and Gentiles. He loved across racial, social, religious, political, monetary, and gender barriers. He would love one group of people, and then they would be shocked to find out that he also loved their most hated enemies. I loved the world so much that I gave him to you so you could see what real love is. And now that he has come, there is no excuse for prejudice. There is no room in a Christian's heart for hatred of any person.

You are my son. I know that you love me. Make that love perfect by giving up all of your little hidden prejudices and hatreds. Give up your stereotypes of those who aren't like you and make an attempt to love as Jesus did. One of the most powerful ways of expressing your love for me is by loving my children the way I do.

The Lover of All Mankind,
>God

== == ==   == == == == == == == == ==

THE PROCESS OF DECREASING AND INCREASING

He who has the bride is the bridegroom; but the friend of the bridegroom, who stands and hears him, rejoices greatly because of the bridegroom's voice. So this joy of mine has been made full. He must increase, but I must decrease.

John — 3:29-30

My Son,

>Every process has to start correctly or else there will be problems. John the Baptist knew the way to start the salvation of the world was to make way for the one who was going to do the saving. He knew that if he stood in the way of that, he would mess things up not only for himself but also for the others Jesus had come to save. So John knew that his own influence had to decrease and Jesus' influence had to increase.

Son, the same thing has to become true in your life. If the process of your redemption is to continue, you have to make way for what I'm doing. Your own agenda has to decrease so that mine can increase. The world places such an emphasis on personal increase that it's hard to see personal decrease as beneficial. But in the spiritual life, the only way to make room for me is to move more of yourself out of the way. So follow John's example, my son, and make way for my plans.

Increasingly More,
>God

LOVE PERFECTED IN YOU

No one has seen God at any time; if we love one another, God abides in us, and His love is perfected in us.

| 1 John | 4:12 |

My Son,

>Sometimes the clearest view of me that someone will see is the way I live in you. You are my walking, talking gospel alive in the world today.

I have made a home in you, and everyone you allow into your life will be welcomed in to see me living there. They will feel the warmth of my Spirit and see the light of my hope calling out on a dark, cold night. They will feel the embrace of my love and smell the fragrance of my grace. All of this is in you because I live in you. And these things will be made perfect in you as you love people and live my welcoming gospel of hope.

Don't miss the opportunity of seeing my love perfected in your life. As you love your neighbor, you are showing my perfect love to the world.

Love Perfected,
>God

== == ==   == == == == == == == == ==

MASTER OF THE BOAT AND THE SEA

Behold, there arose a great storm on the sea, so that the boat was being swamped by the waves; but he was asleep. And they went and woke him, saying, "Save, Lord; we are perishing." And he said to them, "Why are you afraid, O men of little faith?" Then he rose and rebuked the winds and the sea; and there was a great calm. And the men marveled, saying, "What sort of man is this, that even winds and sea obey him?"

Matthew 8:24-27 RSV

My Son,

>Peter was an accomplished fisherman. But even after years of fishing, he had never truly mastered the sea from which he made his living. In the midst of an uncontrollable storm, Peter recognized the uselessness of his knowledge of boats and tides and rigging. To Peter, Jesus was a carpenter, not a master seaman, so he allowed Jesus to grab a nap while the others fished. But when the storm arose, Peter called out to the master of everything. You see, Peter controlled the ship, but Jesus controlled the sea.

Once Jesus was awake, he did what I had sent him to do. He equipped Peter and the disciples with his peace. He calmed the storm that they could not navigate. He entered into Peter's most intimate world and took control.

Will you put me in control of your most intimate world? Making me Lord of every aspect of your life will release in you more peace than you thought possible.

Your Peace,
>God

LOVE'S POSSESSION AND LOVE'S EXPRESSION

Nor does anyone light a lamp and put it under a basket, but on the lampstand, and it gives light to all who are in the house. Let your light shine before men in such a way that they may see your good works, and glorify your Father who is in heaven.

Matthew 5:15-16

My Child,

>There is a difference between knowing how much you love someone and being able to express that love effectively to the other person. Your family and friends need to know how much you love them. But it's hard for them to gauge your love if you don't show it. They need to see it expressed in the way you spend time with them, in what you say to them, in how you treat them.

If I had just dropped my beloved children down into the center of creation and stepped back, they would have had to guess about my love. Instead, I spoke in the Bible and continue to speak to you today. I am always available to spend time with you and listen to you. And the greatest expression of my love was that I laid down the life of my Son, my own flesh and blood.

Go to your loved ones today and tell them that you love them. Give them a hug. Spend time with them. Begin to lay down your own life so that they will know how much you love them. Don't worry if it doesn't come naturally to you at first. Believe me—this is what they need from you. And I will help you express your love.

I love you,
>God

== == ==   == == == == == == == == ==

THE DESIRES OF YOUR HEART

May He give you the desire of your heart.

Psalm 20:4 NIV

My Child,

>From the time you were a little child, whenever you've made a birthday wish and blown out the candles, I've known what you wished for. I've always known what's been most important to you, because it's also been important to me.

I don't want you to feel that the sincere hopes of your heart are bad. It's not a sin to desire what's good and hope for what's great. Placing these things above me is a sin, but desiring them is not.

I am the God who frees you up to dream. The sincere and godly desires of your heart are so important to me. They are a big part of who you are. I have given you these dreams, and I've also given you the abilities and miraculous provision to see them come true.

Your Dad,
>God

== == ==   == == == == == == == == ==

MEET ME IN THE MORNING

In the morning, O LORD, You will hear my voice; in the morning I will order my prayer to You and eagerly watch.

Psalm 5:3

My Child,

>When you wake up in the morning, I'll be waiting. Meet with me in the mornings if you can. Come to me and ask for strength, and I will give it to you. Ask for clarity, and I will clear the junk out of your mind and give you spiritual vision.

I will meet with you, and together we'll tackle the day. When you wake up, say, "Good morning, Father." Have breakfast with me. Share your hopes and fears with me about your day. And then when it's time to go about the jobs of the day, take me with you. We'll do them together. I'll be with you all day long.

Don't run out into your day by yourself. Meet me in the morning, and together we'll make the day the best it can be.

Your Daily Provider,
>God

== == ==   == == == == == == == == ==

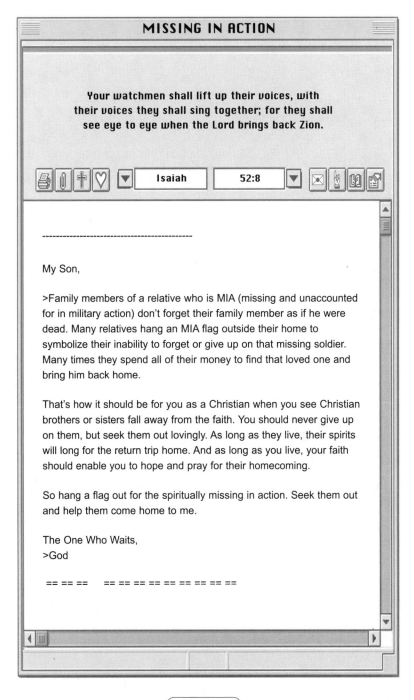

MISSING IN ACTION

Your watchmen shall lift up their voices, with
their voices they shall sing together; for they shall
see eye to eye when the Lord brings back Zion.

Isaiah 52:8

My Son,

>Family members of a relative who is MIA (missing and unaccounted
for in military action) don't forget their family member as if he were
dead. Many relatives hang an MIA flag outside their home to
symbolize their inability to forget or give up on that missing soldier.
Many times they spend all of their money to find that loved one and
bring him back home.

That's how it should be for you as a Christian when you see Christian
brothers or sisters fall away from the faith. You should never give up
on them, but seek them out lovingly. As long as they live, their spirits
will long for the return trip home. And as long as you live, your faith
should enable you to hope and pray for their homecoming.

So hang a flag out for the spiritually missing in action. Seek them out
and help them come home to me.

The One Who Waits,
>God

== == ==   == == == == == == == == ==

MISSION POSSIBLE

Moses said to God, "Who am I that I should go to Pharaoh, and bring the sons of Israel out of Egypt?"

Exodus | **3:11 RSV**

My Son,

>I have created you for great purposes. Sometimes these purposes are going to look as though they're far beyond your reach. But know that if I call you to do something, I didn't dial the wrong number. I know you: your gifts and your faults. And because I know you, I know how to assign to you the job you can accomplish.

After all, it isn't your ability or inability that will affect the ultimate outcome. It's your obedience to me and the way that I supernaturally equip you that will make seemingly impossible missions very possible.

I am choosing to use you in powerful ways. Don't accept my assignment based on how you think you'll do. Accept it based on your faith in what I can and will do through you.

This message will *not* self-destruct in thirty seconds,
>God

== == ==   == == == == == == == == ==

MY CHARACTER DOESN'T CHANGE

Do not err, my beloved brethren. Every good gift and every perfect gift is from above, and cometh down from the Father of lights, with whom is no variableness, neither shadow of turning.

James 1:16-17 KJV

My Son,

>Has your boss ever hinted that he was going to give you a raise and then given it to someone else? Have you ever thought you were the big winner on a promotional quiz only to read the small print and realize the whole thing was a rip-off? Life is full of big promises that don't pay off.

Unlike those here-today, gone-tomorrow promises, my character doesn't change. I don't promise you one thing and then give you something else. I don't rejoice in you only when you're doing great and then turn my back on you when you're in a bad place. I am not two-faced. I am with you all the way, all the time. That's why you can trust me. I am the same yesterday, today, and forever. And I am the solid foundation that will never shift or crumble—the foundation on which you can build your life. Trust in me, my son. I am the truest friend you will ever have and your most dependable ally.

The Totally Reliable,
>God

== == ==   == == == == == == == == ==

MY LOVE

His banner over me is love.

Song of Songs | 2:4 NIV

My Child,

>Who is the person in your life who has loved you through thick and thin? (Your mom, your dad, a grandparent, or a friend?) I love you even more than that person has ever been able to love you. His or her love is like a diamond with only one facet. But my love is a multifaceted gem that reflects my character in every area of your life.

My love is a covering of protection over you. It is a battle cry as I go out against your enemies. My love is the table where you and I sit and share our lives. It is the heart that hears you and truly understands you. My love can't give up on you. It won't turn away. It can't be bought or sold. Nothing can stop my love. My love is perfectly exhibited in Jesus, who proved that my commitment to you cannot be put to death. Through his sacrifice, my love can shine on earth as it does in Heaven. Receive the beauty and value of my love today and let me shine on you.

I love you, my son,
>God

== == ==   == == == == == == == == ==

MY PLACE IN YOUR HEART

**He whose walk is upright fears the Lord, but
he whose ways are devious despises Him.**

Proverbs 14:2 | NIV

My Child,

>Have you ever wondered why sometimes you just don't feel like
spending time with me or being around me? Many times it's because
you've allowed other things to come into your life and distract you.
They could be sinful things, such as greed or lust, or they could be
seemingly harmless hobbies, such as fishing or woodworking. If
you're paying more attention to these competing interests than to me,
they are not harmless at all.

You will always defend what is first in your life at the expense of everything
else. So if you remove me from the first place of honor in your heart,
then I become just one more hindrance to what is really important to
you. And at that point, our love relationship has been compromised.

You are my friend and my son. Have an upright heart that places me
first and is committed to keeping me there.

In Your Heart,
>God

== == ==   == == == == == == == == ==

NO OTHER ARTIST

Now, O Lord, You are our Father, we are the clay, and You our potter; and all of us are the work of Your hand.

| Isaiah | 64:8 |

My Child,

>I am molding you into a unique work of art. There is no one on earth like you. I have particular plans for your life. You don't necessarily need to become the church's ideal of a godly man. You certainly don't need to try and achieve the world's concept of what a mature man or a successful man is. And even your own personal ideas about who you should be can get in the way of my plans. Allowing these other opinions to influence who you become is like letting other artists have a hand in your development. Instead, become the man I want you to be, molded only by my expert eyes and hands.

Bring everything you are into my light and let me give you clarity. Let me set everything in order. I'll show you what to strive for, what to be thankful for, and the things to let go of. I am the potter and you are the clay. Don't let any other artists place their hands on you.

The Perfect Artist,
>God

== == ==   == == == == == == == == ==

PEACE IN THE STORM

Do not fear, for I am with you; do not anxiously look about you, for I am your God. I will strengthen you, surely I will help you, surely I will uphold you with My righteous right hand.

Isaiah 41:10

My Child,

>If you are waiting for peace to come to you as a result of finishing a project, achieving a goal, or checking all the things off your to-do list, then you will continually be disappointed. If you think you'll find peace by changing your job or moving to a quieter neighborhood or taking a vacation to a tranquil ocean setting, you're in for a letdown.

You can get satisfaction from a job well done. You may find a less stressful job. You may relocate to a neighborhood with less traffic or lie on the beach for a week, but the satisfaction you feel is not peace. You can only find peace and contentment in me.

So if you're thinking, *I'll just get through this week and then I'll slow down and have some peace,* then you're off base. I give you peace in the midst of the storm. I'm with you in the midst of the busyness or the noisy neighborhood. Turn to me and have peace right where you are.

Your Prince of Peace,
>God

PICKLES AND TAKING TIME TO TRANSFORM

Purge me with hyssop, and I shall be clean; wash me, and I shall be whiter than snow.

| Psalm | 51:7 KJV |

My Child,

>It takes a long time to make a cucumber into a pickle. You can't just zap it in the microwave. It takes boiling, spices, soaking, pressure, and, most importantly, time. When it's done, you can no longer call it a cucumber. It is now a pickle.

I am bringing you from darkness into light. I am changing you from your old man into my new man. Don't expect a quick fix. The transformation ingredients are already provided, but you have to go through the transformation *process*. First, it takes boiling you down until you are humble and ready to receive. Then you soak in the presence of my Holy Spirit and the seasoning of my Word. It also takes some character-refining pressure and tribulation. And none of this is accomplished overnight.

You are saved in the blink of an eye, but you are transformed over time. Be willing to give me the time to carry out the process of your transformation. I am changing you into who I want you to be (and it's so much more than a pickle!).

Your Transformer,
>God

POWERFUL THINGS IN WEAK PACKAGES

God has chosen the foolish things of the world to shame the wise, and God has chosen the weak things of the world to shame the things which are strong,

| 1 Corinthians | 1:27 |

My Child,

>I've placed a lot of powerful things in weak packages. Moses was a spokesman with a speech impediment. Mary Magdalene was a follower of God who had been a prostitute. Jesus, the King of the world, came as a helpless baby born in a stable.

On the other hand, I've also seen a lot of weakness inside of some very powerful containers. Saul was bigger and stronger than everybody else, but his heart and mind turned weak. Goliath was a giant who was killed by a little boy with a huge heart for me. The Roman Empire ruled the world, but its power couldn't outlast the truth and power of that little baby mentioned above.

You are my son. I don't want you to buy into the lie of the exterior. Don't put your focus on your looks. Don't worry about what people think about you. I have placed powerful things inside you. Let me develop your character, the inner man that only you and I can see.

Your Creator,
>God

REAL MEN CAN FEEL

**Blessed are those who mourn,
for they will be comforted.**

Matthew | 5:4 NIV

My Son,

>Sometimes it's so hard for men to know what they're feeling inside. A lot of men could tell you eighty reasons why they like their favorite sports team, but they couldn't tell you how they really felt when someone close to them died.

Women haven't cornered the market on emotions. Men have emotions too, whether they can express them or not. I want you to know that it's not the sign of a real man to be out of touch with feelings. In fact, if you aren't able to feel and express your feelings to those around you, you will miss out on a lot of what you were created to be. You won't be a great husband to your wife, a good father to your children, a real friend to your friends.

Jesus, the most truly masculine man who ever lived, wept at the loss of his friend Lazarus. He expressed love for his disciples by washing their feet, affirming them, and sharing in their joys and sorrows. You are my son. Don't be fooled by the image of the stoic man. Be free to cry at what hurts and laugh at what makes you happy. I will comfort you in your pain and laugh with you in your joy.

The Lord of Your Emotions,
>God

== == ==   == == == == == == == == ==

RECEIVE CRITICISM HUMBLY

Better is open rebuke than hidden love.

Proverbs | 27:5 NIV

My Son,

>A godly man is confident enough to take criticism. A prideful, immature man feels he needs to be right all the time. Men tend to hate rebuke and spend a lot of energy setting up defenses so they won't have to receive it.

It's okay to be wrong. A man who can learn from his mistakes is a lot better off than someone who spends his life guarding against and covering up his mistakes.

Son, I'm calling you to be a humble man, someone who can admit it when he's wrong and who can acknowledge the fact that sometimes someone else knows more than he does. When you receive constructive criticism, before you feel a need to justify yourself, bring it to me in prayer. I'll show you how you should react and what you should do in response. It will make you a better man.

Your Security,
>God

== == ==   == == == == == == == == ==

RECEIVE THE REVELATION AND KEEP MOVING

No one puts a piece of unshrunk cloth on
an old garment; for the patch tears away
from the garment, and a worse tear is made.

Matthew 9:16

My Son,

>So many times Christians are afraid to try new things. They receive a revelation of me, and they falsely believe that they know all there is to know about me. So they pitch their tent at that place of revelation and stay there.

Unfortunately, then it's hard to get them to move on. I want to say, "Yes, I did show you the truth about that one thing, but there's still so much more to know." But by the time I speak this to them, their tent has become a permanent building, and the revelation has become etched in stone. And when that shrine is finished, there's no room left for new revelation. Suppose Abraham had stayed where I first revealed myself to him. He would never have inherited the promises that were fulfilled as he moved on with me.

Son, you have only seen the smile on my face. There is so much more for me to reveal to you. Don't build a shrine to what you already know of me. Keep your eyes and your heart open to new revelation.

Ever Moving,
>God

RELATIONSHIPS CAN BE PRICKLY

Make my joy complete by being of the same mind, maintaining the same love, united in spirit, intent on one purpose.

Philippians 2:2

My Son,

>Human relationships are kind of like porcupines on a winter night. Porcupines need each other for the warmth, but they keep pricking each other as they move in close. So they back off and readjust and try again, hoping they'll get it right.

People have their own quills of selfishness and pride. They have sharp points of unforgiveness and judgment. As they try to get close to each other, they inevitably encounter the sharper points of each other's personalities. They can either give up and isolate themselves or continue in pursuit of the warmth of fellowship.

You know you need other people in your life. You need their friendship and their company, but if you can't push past their bad points, you will never feel the warmth of real love. Let me help you become less prickly yourself as you reposition yourself to move in again toward fellowship.

The Creator of Closeness,
>God

RISE AND DANCE

"Rise, take up your bed and go home." And he rose and went home. When the crowds saw it, they were afraid, and they glorified God, who had given such authority to men.

| | Matthew | 9:6-8 RSV | |

My Son,

>When Jesus told the paralyzed man to rise up and walk, he walked. And then he was so overwhelmed with gratitude that he rejoiced.

Being grateful for your healing isn't standing up and asking Jesus why he allowed you to be lame all of those years. It's rising up and dancing down the street, praising me for my blessing. Do you have the joy of gratitude for what I've given you? Or do you question why I haven't given you what you feel you deserve?

Rejoice in all the things that you have. Realize that I am healing your heart. Rise up and dance.

Your Healer,
>God

== == ==   == == == == == == == == ==

SEEK AND YOU WILL FIND

Ask, and it will be given to you; seek, and
you will find; knock, and it will be opened to you.
For everyone who asks receives, and he who seeks
finds, and to him who knocks it will be opened.

Matthew   7:7-8

My Child,

>There is no promise of finding the truth for those who don't and
won't seek it. If you have a phony external faith that simply denies
any internal doubts that you harbor, then you are unlikely to really
know the truth. It's time to get honest with yourself and with me. Bring
your doubts out of the closet and into the light. Let's talk about them.
Let's search the scriptures together. Let's seek the counsel of sound
Biblical scholars. Faith does not mean bravely denying any real
doubts you have; it means seeking the answers and attempting to
bring a real resolution to the dissonance of that doubt.

If you will seek the answers fearlessly, then you will find me. If you
will stop pretending to have a bullet-proof external faith, then you will
have some amazing opportunities to build a solid, internal faith. I am
the truth. Seek and you will find.

Your Father,
>God

== == ==   == == == == == == == == ==

SEEK ME FIRST

Seek ye first the kingdom of God, and his righteousness; and all these things shall be added unto you.

Matthew | 6:33 KJV

My Child,

>If you seek the things that you think you need, then you will live a life of frustration, second-guessing, and anxiety. But if you seek me first, then everything you need will be added to you.

If you are walking forward with your eyes looking straight at me, then the things that you need will meet you along that straight path. But if you run here and there looking for all the things you think you need, your eyes will be off of me, and you will get lost.

When you have the peace of knowing that you are seeking me first, then every decision will be easier. Your priorities will be clear. You will worry less. You will be closer to me. You can rest in my promise that I will give you everything you need.

Your First Priority,
>God

== == ==   == == == == == == == == ==

BLESS OTHERS WITH YOUR BLESSINGS

Now we who are strong ought to bear the weaknesses of those without strength and not just please ourselves.

Romans 15:1

My Son,

>You were delivered from sin and selfishness through Jesus' selfless sacrifice. Now that you were bought with that price, you can't continue to act selfishly. Live your life with open hands.

For example, if a beggar asks you to give him three bucks for a meal, do it. Your whole life could be taken in the next minute. Nothing is yours to keep. It's all on loan from me, so don't deny others who are in need. I've blessed you not only to provide for yourself, my son, but also to share with others in need. Seek me on how to use your blessings to bless others.

The Father of All Blessings,
>God

== == ==   == == == == == == == == ==

SEND OUT THE GIFTS

Like clouds and wind without rain is a man
who boasts of a gift he does not give.

Proverbs | **25:14 RSV**

My Son,

>It's one thing to have gifts and a very different thing to use those gifts for the reason they were given. You know what abilities you have, and you know that I can use them. But that isn't enough.

I didn't make you a warehouse for good stuff just to have you lock the door and hide the key. I have set those good things inside of you with specific shipping addresses on them. They're supposed to go out to others in my world.

I encourage you to open up the warehouse of your gifts and start shipping them to my destinations. As you do, I'll keep you stocked with a continuous supply of inventory, and you'll have many satisfied customers.

The Giver of All Gifts,
>God

== == ==   == == == == == == == == ==

STEP INTO THE LIGHT

**In Him was life, and the life was the Light of men.
The light shines in the darkness, and the darkness
did not comprehend it.**

| John | 1:4-5 |

My Child,

>Have you ever wondered why some people get a little uncomfortable or fearful when you start talking about me? Many times, it's because when my light shines on a person, it shines into every dark corner and closet of the heart. I don't shine only on the parts of a person that they've worked so hard to present as shiny and acceptable. I bring everything into the light.

A man who has stepped totally into the light has nothing to fear. That man has already been exposed and seen himself for who he really is: a child of mine, and a sinner in need of a Savior. Once that man receives my salvation, he's on the road to becoming who I've created him to be.

Have you stepped totally into the light? Take my hand and let me make you fearless. In the purity of my light, I will show you who I've created you to be.

Step into the light,
>God

GET OUT OF THE BOAT

In the fourth watch of the night he came to them, walking on the sea. . . . And Peter answered him, "Lord, if it is you, bid me come to you on the water." He said, "Come." So Peter got out of the boat and walked on the water and came to Jesus.

Matthew 14: | 25, 28-29 RSV

My Child,

>Peter knew boats. He felt comfortable and safe on the sea. But when he saw Jesus walking on the water, he knew he was dealing with a whole new challenge. In the same way, I am calling you out of your comfort zone. I am calling you into a place where you'll have to trust me totally in order to operate. Don't be afraid. This is where the adventure lies.

Sometimes, even when you're an active Christian, you can get comfortable in your element and forget that there is so much more beyond your experience. If you've ever thought, *I'm just not comfortable doing that,* it's time to think again.

Just like Peter, you have to know the one who calls you. Then you can step out into that new area with confidence. Even when the winds kick up and you feel as if you're sinking, keep walking. I'm moving you out of your "small boat" of expectations onto the vast sea of my will.

Take my hand,
>God

== == ==   == == == == == == == == ==

STRESS IS A STATE OF MIND

You will go out with joy and be led forth with peace; the mountains and the hills will break forth into shouts of joy before you, and all the trees of the field will clap their hands.

Isaiah   55:12

My Child,

>I never give you more than you can handle in one day. It's easy to stress out and worry about all that you've got on your plate. But the truth is, you'll accomplish what you can accomplish, and the rest will wait till you have time to handle it.

Stress doesn't come from the number or variety of things you have to do. It comes from the way you let those things affect you. Two men can carry the exact same workload. One man will stress out, whereas the other will work peacefully and well. It all depends on the attitude and spirit with which the work is approached.

I have called you to a life of peace, my son. Giving stress the upper hand in your life is making it an idol. I can give you the attitude and abilities needed to handle the load as you walk in my peace.

Your Deliverance from Stress,
>God

== == ==   == == == == == == == == ==

THE BADGE OF INDEPENDENCE

If all were a single organ, where would the body be?

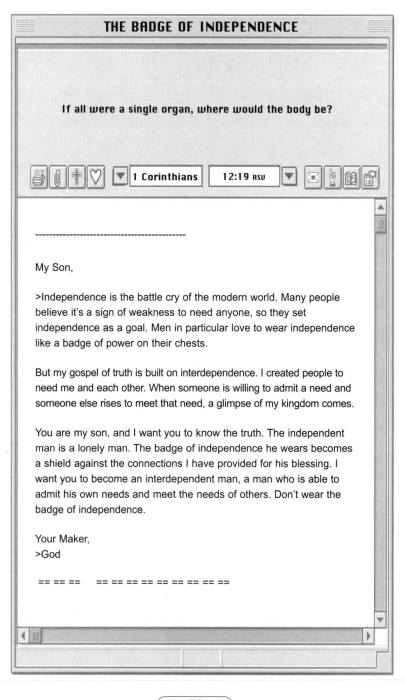

1 Corinthians · 12:19 RSV

My Son,

>Independence is the battle cry of the modern world. Many people believe it's a sign of weakness to need anyone, so they set independence as a goal. Men in particular love to wear independence like a badge of power on their chests.

But my gospel of truth is built on interdependence. I created people to need me and each other. When someone is willing to admit a need and someone else rises to meet that need, a glimpse of my kingdom comes.

You are my son, and I want you to know the truth. The independent man is a lonely man. The badge of independence he wears becomes a shield against the connections I have provided for his blessing. I want you to become an interdependent man, a man who is able to admit his own needs and meet the needs of others. Don't wear the badge of independence.

Your Maker,
>God

== == ==   == == == == == == == == ==

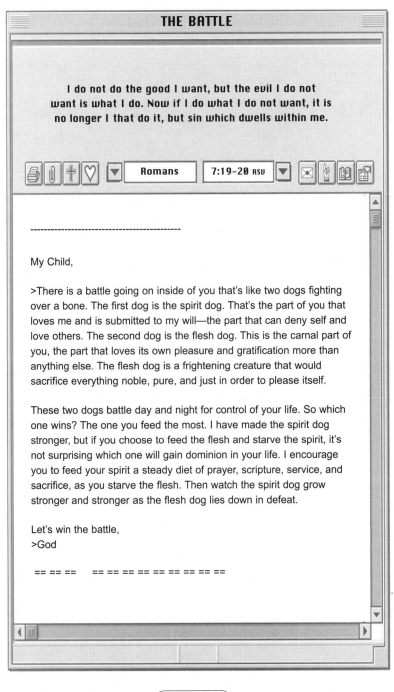

THE BATTLE

I do not do the good I want, but the evil I do not want is what I do. Now if I do what I do not want, it is no longer I that do it, but sin which dwells within me.

Romans 7:19-20 RSV

My Child,

>There is a battle going on inside of you that's like two dogs fighting over a bone. The first dog is the spirit dog. That's the part of you that loves me and is submitted to my will—the part that can deny self and love others. The second dog is the flesh dog. This is the carnal part of you, the part that loves its own pleasure and gratification more than anything else. The flesh dog is a frightening creature that would sacrifice everything noble, pure, and just in order to please itself.

These two dogs battle day and night for control of your life. So which one wins? The one you feed the most. I have made the spirit dog stronger, but if you choose to feed the flesh and starve the spirit, it's not surprising which one will gain dominion in your life. I encourage you to feed your spirit a steady diet of prayer, scripture, service, and sacrifice, as you starve the flesh. Then watch the spirit dog grow stronger and stronger as the flesh dog lies down in defeat.

Let's win the battle,
>God

== == ==   == == == == == == == == ==

THE BEAST OF MATERIALISM

He said to them, "Take heed, and beware of all covetousness; for a man's life does not consist in the abundance of his possessions."

| Luke | 12:15 RSV |

My Son,

>Why do people continue to place their hope in things? They jump from purchase to purchase, feeling temporarily satisfied by each new possession. But materialism is a beast with an insatiable appetite, and it lives within men.

For example, a materialistic man with a miserable life and an old station wagon knows in his materialistic heart that if he can just get enough money or credit to buy a sleek sports car, then he will be happy. His desire eats at his heart and pushes him into debt or into overworking in order to buy the car. But when he gets it, nothing has actually changed, other than his mode of transportation. Now he is just a man with a miserable life and a sports car.

Son, material possessions do not bring happiness. They just bring a need for more storage space. Seek your contentment in me alone.

The Love of Great Value,
>God

== == ==   == == == == == == == == ==

THE BIG EVENT

I have no one else of kindred spirit who will genuinely be concerned for your welfare. For they all seek after their own interests, not those of Christ Jesus. But you know of his proven worth, that he served with me in the furtherance of the gospel like a child serving his father.

🖨 📎 ✝ ♡ ▼ **Philippians** | **2:20-22** ▼ ⊠ ✋ 📖 📝

My Son,

>Many men are great at the big event. They can plan a family vacation perfectly and can foot the bill for a great date night. This is admirable, but many of those same men are failures at day-to-day living and loving in their families.

Big events are great, but day-to-day living is so much more important. It means turning off the television and listening to your children and your wife. It means choosing to read a bedtime story rather than the newspaper or magazine you had been planning to look at. It means telling your family that you love them, rather than expecting them to know it just because you took them to Disney World that time two years ago.

So here's the challenge. Try being the hero of the big events, the little events, and all the time in between. That's the kind of hero I am.

Creator of the Biggest Events Ever,
>God

== == ==   == == == == == == == == ==

THE BLESSING OF SUFFERING

We also rejoice in our sufferings, because we know that suffering produces perseverance; perseverance, character; and character hope.

| | Romans | 5:3–4 NIV | |

My Child,

>The world is so obsessed with avoiding any form of pain or suffering. If your head hurts a little, take a pill. If you need to cry, don't do it in front of others. But suffering is not always bad. Sometimes it is the very tool I can use to make you into a man of character.

Sometimes the richest blessing can come out of hardship and suffering. This isn't because I'm cruel. It's because I have deeper things in mind for you than your own comfort. Medical surgery involves pain and recovery, but that shouldn't make you avoid a procedure that is in your best interests.

So when pain or suffering comes your way, rather than trying desperately to avoid it, pray about it. If I want to use that difficult thing to refine you, embrace it and welcome it. Then you will see what it is to be a man of character, refined by the pain of life rather than avoiding it.

Your Father,
>God

== == ==   == == == == == == == == ==

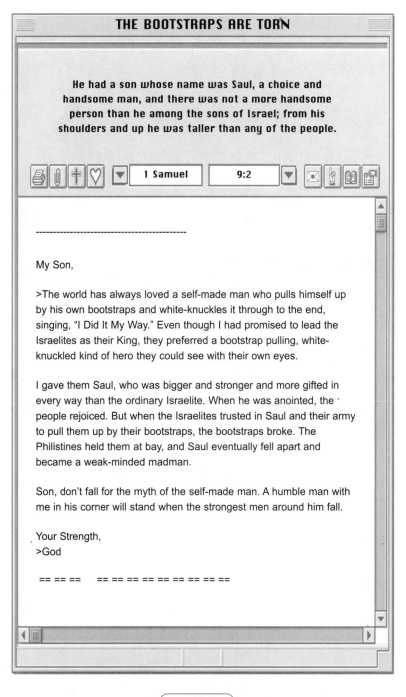

THE BOOTSTRAPS ARE TORN

He had a son whose name was Saul, a choice and handsome man, and there was not a more handsome person than he among the sons of Israel; from his shoulders and up he was taller than any of the people.

| | 1 Samuel | 9:2 | |

My Son,

>The world has always loved a self-made man who pulls himself up by his own bootstraps and white-knuckles it through to the end, singing, "I Did It My Way." Even though I had promised to lead the Israelites as their King, they preferred a bootstrap pulling, white-knuckled kind of hero they could see with their own eyes.

I gave them Saul, who was bigger and stronger and more gifted in every way than the ordinary Israelite. When he was anointed, the people rejoiced. But when the Israelites trusted in Saul and their army to pull them up by their bootstraps, the bootstraps broke. The Philistines held them at bay, and Saul eventually fell apart and became a weak-minded madman.

Son, don't fall for the myth of the self-made man. A humble man with me in his corner will stand when the strongest men around him fall.

Your Strength,
>God

== == ==   == == == == == == == == ==

THE GIFT

**A man's gift makes room for him
and brings him before great men.**

| Proverbs | 18:16 |

My Son,

>Imagine that your best friend sent you a new tool that he had seen
on TV. This tool could replace every handheld or electric tool ever
known. It could convert air into clean burning gasoline. It could help
people get along with one another. It could slice and dice your food,
bring home the bacon, fry it in the pan—you get the idea.

Do you think you would be content to keep that tool in the box out in
the tool shed and visit it once a week? Of course you wouldn't. You
would tear that box open and put it to use.

Son, I am the ultimate resource for your life. It's time to break open
the gift and start letting me affect everything around you. Don't just
visit me at church once a week. Take me home and put me to work in
your world.

The Gift,
>God

== == ==   == == == == == == == == ==

THE END OF YOUR ROPE

**Blessed are the poor in spirit:
for theirs is the kingdom of heaven.**

Matthew | 5:3 KJV

My Son,

>You are blessed when you are at the end of your rope, because if
you have reached the end of your own abilities and you stand humbly
before me, that's when the kingdom of heaven is truly yours.

When there is less of you, there is more room for me.

So many times my children feel that they have to present me with
some sort of proof of how spiritual they are and what good Christians
they've become. I would rather find a man who knows he's spiritually
bankrupt and wants a relationship with me. That man is empty and
available for the filling of my Holy Spirit.

Will you let me bring you to the end of yourself? Will you hunger and
thirst for me as a starving man hungers for food? Will you let me give
you the heavenly inheritance of the spiritually poor?

Your Heavenly Father,
>God

== == ==   == == == == == == == == ==

THE GOOD NEWS

The next day he saw Jesus coming to him and said, "Behold, the Lamb of God who takes away the sin of the world!"

John　　1:29

My Child,

>In the beginning I created man to be in a perfect relationship with me—to walk with me in the Garden. But I also gave him this option: He could choose me and my way or choose to be in charge of his own life. He chose himself over me, and as a result man spent centuries striving toward, but never quite reaching, the goal of his existence—to live in a right relationship with me.

My people, the Israelites, offered up sacrifices and sin offerings trying to bridge the gap between them and me, but that blood covering was only temporary. They still felt the distance between us. Then I sent Jesus to earth, and he laid his life down as the perfect, once-and-for-all sin offering. The distance was dissolved between Heaven and earth for those who would only accept his sacrifice. Eden was reinstated. Now I walk with men again and abide in their hearts. Believe it!

The Good News Bearer,
>God

== == ==　　== == == == == == == == ==

THE GOOD, THE BAD, AND THE UGLY

First clean the inside of the cup and of the dish, so that the outside of it may become clean also.

Matthew	23:26

My Child,

>Many people spend all their time and energy trying to make a great-looking external person who will be acceptable and pleasing to others and also to me. The outside is not all that interests me. I'm interested in everything: the good, the bad, and the ugly.

If you paint a house perfectly on the outside, but leave the inside with rotten wood and no amenities, then the house doesn't bless the people who live there. It only blesses the neighbors and the passers-by. I live inside of you, and *so do you*. You are a temple for my Holy Spirit. It's time to stop doing all the exterior work to make you appear good to others. It's time to start blessing me by cleaning yourself up on the inside. Appearing holy and being holy are two very different things.

So, let's get started on the inside!

The One Who Lives in You,
>God

== == ==   == == == == == == == == ==

THE GREATEST

Therefore when the people saw the sign which He had performed, they said, "This is truly the Prophet who is to come into the world." So Jesus, perceiving that they were intending to come and take Him by force to make Him king, withdrew again to the mountain by Himself alone.

| John | 6:14–15 |

My Child,

>The Jewish people wanted Jesus to gallop in on a white horse with full armor, unite Israel, and conquer Rome. What He did instead was to carry out my perfect plan. He cared about people, even very unlovely people. He prayed. He understood human pain. He took the time to really listen. He walked the slow road to the cross.

When he rose from the grave, he didn't reveal himself to kings and rulers. Instead, he spent time with the people he loved, healing their broken hearts and giving them gifts that they would need to survive.

My son, this is how I want you to live. I want you to pour yourself into the ones you love because you love them. Don't seek to be the world's greatest. Just seek to do my will, and that will make you great in my sight.

Your Father,
>God

== == ==   == == == == == == == == ==

THE HOPE OF THE WORLD

Heal the sick, raise the dead, cleanse lepers, cast out demons. You received without paying, give without pay.

Matthew   10:8 RSV

My Child,

>The world is a broken place full of hurting people and seemingly hopeless situations. This is not the way I created it. But since man fell from the grace I provided in the beginning, all kinds of brokenness (suffering, sorrow, poverty, pain, and death) came into the world.

But through Jesus Christ, there is hope for restoration in the midst of all the brokenness. Because you follow Jesus, now you are the hope of the world. You are the hands and feet and heart of Christ on earth. And the heart of Christ does not give up. It sacrifices everything it has to reach out and heal the world.

Don't be discouraged by what seem to be overwhelming odds. You can't save the world by yourself, and you can't do it in a day. But you can do your part. With my Spirit in you, you can make a difference—one heart, one life, one day, one person, one challenge at a time.

Your Hope,
>God

== == ==   == == == == == == == == ==

THE JOY OF MY PRESENCE

In Your presence is fullness of joy; in Your right hand there are pleasures forever.

| Psalm | 16:11 |

My Son,

>Sometimes it would be hard to convince an unbeliever that you serve a loving God based on the somber expression on your face. I didn't create you to walk around in sackcloth and ashes, frowning at the world. I set you free for freedom! Yes, there is a time for weeping and repentance, but it isn't all the time. Give it a rest.

If you feel as if your joy has been sacrificed for a religious idol of falsely somber piety, I say, "Rise up and be free." Let my joy start a celebration in your heart. Laugh out loud. Dance as King David did. Sing with the angels. Here in my presence is true joy that fills the heart. The pleasure of my company is not temporary. It is ongoing and everlasting, and you need not wait for Heaven to enter in. Come and be filled today.

Your Joyful Father,
>God

== == ==   == == == == == == == == ==

THE LAST-MINUTE LIFESTYLE

**Let the king and Haman come tomorrow
to the dinner which I will prepare for them,
and *tomorrow* I will do as the king has said.**

Esther 5:8 RSV

My Son,

>In the same way that skydivers and mountain climbers become addicted to an adrenaline rush, some people get addicted to procrastination. Those who are hooked love the last-minute rush of excitement and the challenge of taking it to the wire. But they end up getting sick of the unnecessary pressure and disorder in their lives.

Procrastination is the curse of an unordered life. But if you place your life under my authority, it will have my order. Think about it. What if Jesus had procrastinated in laying down his life for you? Every move in his life was perfectly timed and submitted. In the submitted life, there can be no last-minute adrenaline addiction. There is only daily submission and the resulting peace.

Sound like a tall order? I am not waiting until the last minute to help you in this area of your life. If you have become addicted to the last-minute lifestyle, bring it to me in prayer, and I will begin to order your life. I will give you peace and productivity that the procrastination addict will never know.

The Creator of Perfect Order,
>God

== == ==   == == == == == == == == ==

THE MARK OF THE MASTER

Those whom He foreknew, He also predestined to become conformed to the image of His Son, so that He would be the firstborn among many brethren.

| Romans | 8:29 |

My Son,

>Historically, master artisans had apprentices who served them for a number of years. While serving under the master, the apprentice was to mark every piece of work he did with the symbol of the master's workshop.

Since you became mine, you are in my service; now you are my apprentice. Are you seeking to leave my mark or your own on this world? When you do something, there is no denying that it is the work of your own hands. But it should leave the imprint of Christ rather than the mark of your own need for recognition.

Submit yourself to my service for life. Let the work of your hands bear my signature, and the world will marvel at the work you do in my name.

Your Master,
>God

== == ==   == == == == == == == == ==

THE MORAL BUY-OUT SCHEME

Be sure of this, that if the head of the house had known at what time of the night the thief was coming, he would have been on the alert and would not have allowed his house to be broken into.

Matthew 24:43

My Child,

>When Satan takes over someone's life, people usually picture it as a hostile takeover. They picture the conquered person signing over his life in one bold stroke on a "life transfer" contract, and then the deed is done.

It usually doesn't happen this way. It's more like this: Satan buys up shares of stock in someone's life. The person thinks, *Oh, a share here, a compromise there—I'm still in control.* But if this continues over a period of time, pretty soon Satan owns a controlling interest in someone's life. And the way Satan exercises those stock options is to turn that bought-out person away from me.

You are my son, and I would never want you to compromise your life. Be aware of every bit of moral and spiritual stock you hold. Don't compromise on even one share. Be sold out to me.

The Chairman of Your Board,
>God

== == ==   == == == == == == == == ==

THE PROUD AND THE MEEK

**Blessed are the meek,
for they will inherit the earth.**

| Matthew | 5:5 NIV |

My Son,

>The proud will not inherit the earth. Even if they hold every major office and head up every major corporation, they will never inherit true riches. Only the humble will be given the real power.

The Jewish people wanted Jesus to be a mighty warrior, a human deliverer from Roman rule. Instead, he was a servant leader. He hung out with all the "wrong" people, washed the feet of his own followers, touched the lepers, and had compassion on the very Roman guards who took his life. But Jesus ultimately inherited total rule over Heaven and earth by humbly drinking the cup that I handed him.

Even though many times it seems that the squeaky wheel gets the grease and the obnoxious guy gets the promotion, you need to have the heavenly perspective. Follow after Jesus. Be assured that if you allow yourself to become like him, you will inherit more riches than you can conceive.

Your Father,
>God

THE ROCK THAT CRUMBLED INTO A FOUNDATION

The Lord turned and looked at Peter. And Peter remembered the word of the Lord, how he had said to him, "Before the cock crows today, you will deny me three times." And he went out and wept bitterly.

Luke 22:61–62 RSV

My Child,

>Just because I speak a hard word to you doesn't mean I'm finished with you. Just because you mess up doesn't mean my plans for your life come to a screeching halt.

Peter did the ultimate thing to hurt me; he denied ever knowing me— not once, but three times. I had spent three very close years with him. He had seen me heal the sick and raise the dead. He had walked with me on the water and seen me transfigured on the mountaintop. He was slated to be a mighty rock for my kingdom. But when pressed upon, this rock crumbled into pieces and lost all hope.

But Peter still became the rock on which I built my church. He still became a spiritual powerhouse for me. He found out what I want you to know. When you fall to pieces, I am the God who can put you back together. I have marvelous plans for your life. When you mess up, let me pick you up and help you move on.

Your Strength,
>God

THE SACRIFICE AND THE REST

David said, "The LORD God of Israel has given rest
to His people, and He dwells in Jerusalem forever.
Also, the Levites will no longer need to carry the
tabernacle and all its utensils for its service."

1 Chronicles **23:25–26**

My Son,

>I have set you free from the burden of having to get yourself into
heaven. You no longer have to offer sacrifices for your sins. You no
longer have to worry about carrying the articles of religion around,
trying to buy your way into the kingdom with good deeds. No one is
good enough to enter Heaven based on his own works.

If there's one thing you should know by now, it's that you're not
perfect. But Jesus was, and that's where things changed for you and
all of mankind. He became the one-time sacrifice so that you could be
with me forever. Because of that, I dwell not only in the ark of the
covenant or in Jerusalem; I dwell in the heart and presence of
everyone who receives the sacrifice of my Son.

Put your hope in nothing but the sacrifice of Jesus. Stop trying to
carry your own salvation. Lay down your life for my purposes, and
you will find your rest in me.

Your Sacrifice of Love,
>God

== == ==   == == == == == == == == ==

YOU ARE A SPIRITUAL BEING

We know that if the earthly tent which is our house is torn down, we have a building from God, a house not made with hands, eternal in the heavens. For indeed in this house we groan, longing to be clothed with our dwelling from heaven.

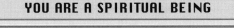 **2 Corinthians** **5:1-2**

My Son,

>Many people who have an encounter with me tend to say that they had a "spiritual experience." But mankind was actually created to live in this spiritual realm, constantly encountering me.

Since you know me, I want you to have a perspective change about the place of the spiritual in your life. You are not a human being having a spiritual experience. You are a spiritual being having a human experience. Even though your temporary mailing address is here on earth, ultimately you are from Heaven and will return to live there in the spiritual realm for eternity. If you seek me with a lifestyle of worship, you can begin right now to encounter the spiritual life you were made for.

Your Creator,
>God

== == ==   == == == == == == == == ==

THE WHOLE OF YOU

Remember now, O Lord, I beseech You, how I have walked before You in truth and with a whole heart and have done what is good in Your sight.

| | 2 Kings | 20:3 | |

My Son,

>Unless you give me all of you, you will never be complete. Don't just hand me the parts of you that you think I want to have, the parts you feel are acceptable. Hand me everything.

Only in my hands can you be made whole. So everything you hold back from me will remain fragmented and unhealed. As long as you hold on to guilt, shame, or embarrassment, Satan will always have a bit in your spiritual mouth and will be able to lead you away from me.

I know who you really are, and I'm crazy about you. I ask you to hand me all of your brokenness and let me make you whole. You are safe with me.

Making You Whole,
>God

== == ==   == == == == == == == == ==

THERE AND HERE

Herein is love, not that we loved God,
but that he loved us.

1 John   4:10 KJV

My Child,

>I chose you before you chose me. I loved you before you ever
decided to love me back. I put a plan in motion for your redemption
before you ever thought about your own salvation. Before you felt the
pain, my healing was available. Even when you felt as if I was a
million miles away, I had my arms around you. In the most painful
time in your life, I was there, holding you. And the times when it all fell
apart, I was the only one who could put it back together.

It fills me with joy that you have come home. Now you can know me
as you never could before. You can know how near I am and hear the
songs I've sung about you all along. Now we can walk together, and I
can show you the places I've always wanted you to see. We can talk
together and share our lives together. I've been here for you all along.
It feels good to have you here with me at last.

The One Who First Loved You,
>God

== == ==   == == == == == == == == ==

THOSE DAYS

**To the praise of the glory of His grace, which
He freely bestowed on us in the Beloved.**

| Ephesians | 1:6 |

My Son,

>Sometimes you just have one of those days. You know what I'm talking about. Everything seems to be going against you, and you can't seem to do anything right. You lock your keys in your car. You curse at the guy who pulls out in front of you in traffic. You're late for work, and you just don't seem to get anything accomplished. You come home at the end of the day feeling like a big loser, and you crawl into bed feeling unlovable. I want you to know something. I love you just as much on one of those days as I do on a day when you feel as if you've done everything right.

You are my son, and I couldn't love you any more or any less. Don't feel as if a bad day separates you from me. Instead, let me love you through those days.

Lord of Every Day,
>God

== == ==   == == == == == == == == ==

TIME

**For where your treasure is,
there your heart will be also.**

| Matthew | 6:21 NIV |

My Child,

>I know you have heard it said that no man at the end of his life wishes that he had spent more time at the office. Love is expressed most effectively through time. So if you want to know where your heart is, look at where you spend most of your time.

Your time is best spent on your loved ones. Time spent with your children is like gold deposited in the bank with the highest interest rate. This is not only true for their sake but for your sake. I am using your family to change you into the kind of man that I want you to be. I am making you unselfish, and I am giving you a Christlike love for others. I know that sometimes it's a lot easier to go to work or to go fishing than to spend focused time with your family. But the joy you receive from knowing that you are blessing your wife and being a great dad to your kids will far outweigh any "sacrifices" you make. Time is more precious than any other measurable item you have on earth. Spend it wisely.

Creator of Time,
>God

== == ==   == == == == == == == == ==

DON'T NARROW YOUR EXPECTATIONS

**Oh that You would bless me indeed
and enlarge my border.**

| | 1 Chronicles | 4:10 | |

My Son,

>I don't want you to narrow your expectations of life. I am calling you to do miraculous things for me, if you will only believe. I am calling you to step out and try something so impossible that if I'm not in it, it is doomed to fail.

Christians who play it safe will live a safe, manicured life. But Christians who believe in my miraculous abilities will see amazing things occur. You are my son, and I have those things in store for you. Step out in faith and answer my call, especially if it seems to be outside the box of your narrow expectations.

Your Miraculous Father,
>God

== == ==   == == == == == == == == ==

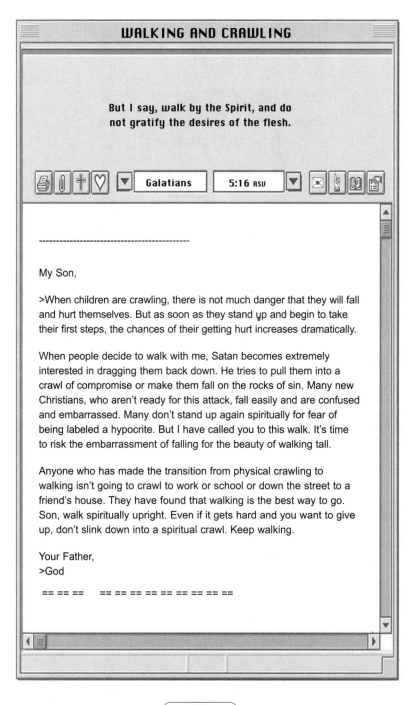

WALKING AND CRAWLING

**But I say, walk by the Spirit, and do
not gratify the desires of the flesh.**

Galatians | 5:16 RSV

My Son,

>When children are crawling, there is not much danger that they will fall
and hurt themselves. But as soon as they stand up and begin to take
their first steps, the chances of their getting hurt increases dramatically.

When people decide to walk with me, Satan becomes extremely
interested in dragging them back down. He tries to pull them into a
crawl of compromise or make them fall on the rocks of sin. Many new
Christians, who aren't ready for this attack, fall easily and are confused
and embarrassed. Many don't stand up again spiritually for fear of
being labeled a hypocrite. But I have called you to this walk. It's time
to risk the embarrassment of falling for the beauty of walking tall.

Anyone who has made the transition from physical crawling to
walking isn't going to crawl to work or school or down the street to a
friend's house. They have found that walking is the best way to go.
Son, walk spiritually upright. Even if it gets hard and you want to give
up, don't slink down into a spiritual crawl. Keep walking.

Your Father,
>God

== == ==   == == == == == == == == ==

WELCOME THE PRODIGALS

He said to him, "Son, you are always with me,
and all that is mine is yours. It was fitting
to make merry and be glad, for this your brother
was dead, and is alive; he was lost, and is found."

| Luke | 15:31-32 RSV |

Dear Child,

>I've always loved you, son. I am proud of the work you've done and the work you are doing. I'm pleased with your good heart and your willing service. But I don't want you to get so caught up in being the good son that you miss my heart for the prodigal son who is returning to me.

He may have been gone for a long time, wasting the gifts I've given him. He may smell bad or dress funny. He may have picked up some bad habits while he was gone. He may not look like you, think like you, or act like you.

But when he is ready to come home, I want you to run with me to greet him. I want you to rejoice in killing the fatted calf and making this stranger welcome in our home, because it's his home too. It's always been prepared for him just as it was for you. Let's welcome my prodigals together, my son.

Your Father,
>God

== == ==   == == == == == == == == ==

WHAT TRULY FILLS

Blessed are those who hunger and thirst for righteousness, for they will be filled.

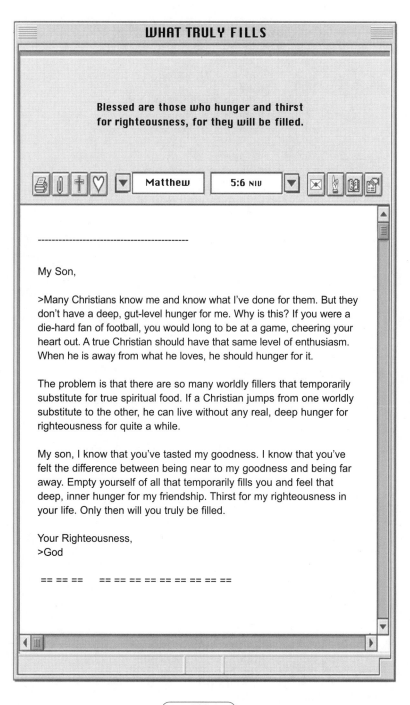

Matthew 5:6 NIV

My Son,

>Many Christians know me and know what I've done for them. But they don't have a deep, gut-level hunger for me. Why is this? If you were a die-hard fan of football, you would long to be at a game, cheering your heart out. A true Christian should have that same level of enthusiasm. When he is away from what he loves, he should hunger for it.

The problem is that there are so many worldly fillers that temporarily substitute for true spiritual food. If a Christian jumps from one worldly substitute to the other, he can live without any real, deep hunger for righteousness for quite a while.

My son, I know that you've tasted my goodness. I know that you've felt the difference between being near to my goodness and being far away. Empty yourself of all that temporarily fills you and feel that deep, inner hunger for my friendship. Thirst for my righteousness in your life. Only then will you truly be filled.

Your Righteousness,
>God

WHO DO YOU SAY I AM?

Not everyone who says to Me, "Lord, Lord," will
enter the kingdom of heaven, but he who does
the will of My Father who is in heaven will enter.

Matthew **7:21**

My Child,

>Who do you say I am? If you say that I'm your Lord and King, do
you say it with your mouth, or do you say it with your life? Which
speaks louder?

If you claim that I'm your Lord, you'll do my will. If you say that I'm
your King, you'll let me rule in your life, rather than ruling yourself. If
you say that I am the Messiah (the Savior), you'll let me save you. If
you say that I'm your Shepherd, you'll follow me.

Don't let your mouth write checks that your actions aren't willing to
pay. Who do you say I am?

Your Lord, King, Savior, and Shepherd,
>God

== == ==   == == == == == == == == ==

WHO IS TO JUDGE?

Accept him whose faith is weak.

Romans | 14:1 NIV

My Son,

>Do you set yourself up as judge over other Christians? It's my job to judge my children with holy justice. Your job is to love and accept your brothers and sisters and to encourage them in their faith.

If you feel you have some insight that would benefit your brother or sister, you can lovingly share that insight. But there's a difference between really wanting a brother or a sister to know the truth and your need to feel that you're right or better than someone else.

Your job is to encourage and not to judge. Leave the sorting out to me.

The Fair Judge,
>God

== == ==   == == == == == == == == ==

WHO YOU REALLY ARE

Thus says the LORD, Israel is my first-born son.

| | Exodus | 4:22 RSV | |

My Son,

>The world sees identity as what you do rather than who you are. Most men see themselves as their profession (a lawyer, a painter, or a schoolteacher). Their sense of self is based primarily on occupation or interests. No matter how natural your work feels, no matter how gifted you are at it or how much money and acclaim it brings you, it isn't who you are.

The beauty of your true identity is best expressed in the statement "my child." The knowledge that you are a wonderfully and carefully created masterpiece, made by my own hands, is the basis of your identity. You are the son of your parents, the friend to mankind, the lover of your loved ones, and my minister to the world.

How you make a living or how you spend your leisure time does not define you. You are my child. Find your identity in me.

Your Creator,
>God

== == ==   == == == == == == == == ==

WORK IS A BLESSING

The LORD God took the man, and put him into the garden of Eden to dress it and to keep it.

Genesis 2:15 KJV

My Child,

>Work was given to men by me in order to bless them. It is *not* a result of the fall of Adam that men have to work. The fall just made work harder to do. But work was there in the beginning, in the Garden when I walked with man.

If you work for a living, consider yourself blessed. I am using that work to refine your character. I'm able to use difficult people and situations, deadlines and challenges, to give life and breath to your Christianity. I'm using little situations at work to build lasting honesty and integrity.

I encourage you, my son, not to scoff at work. Don't live for the weekends, and don't live for retirement. There are fewer lessons to learn on the golf course than in the work place. Let me give you the right attitude about your job. A child who receives everything without co-laboring with his parent remains childish. Work is a blessing, my son. Rejoice in it.

Your Loving Father,
>God

== == ==   == == == == == == == == ==

WORSHIP IS NOT A SPECTATOR SPORT

**Love the Lord your God with all your heart and
with all your soul and with all your strength and with
all your mind; and, love your neighbor as yourself.**

Luke　　10:27 NIV

My Son,

>When you go to see a sporting event, all you have to do is buy a
ticket. You could also choose to buy assorted foods that would give
you heartburn, but that and anything else you chose to do in the
stands would not have an effect on the game.

The worship experience is different. Your showing up is only the
beginning. The two main players on the field of worship are you and
me. Even though it seems as if the pastor and the worship leader are
the main players, they're not. They know that the worship experience
is about my meeting with you. That's what they are there to encourage.

So come with your heart right and ready to go. Give me 110 percent
of your worship. Pray like you mean it. Wrestle with me about things
that are bothering you. Seek me with all of your heart, and you will
find me. Worship is not a spectator sport. So don't come to watch.
Come to play!

I'll meet you on the field,
>God

== == ==   == == == == == == == == ==

YOU ARE MY WORK OF ART

I will give thanks to You, for I am fearfully and wonderfully made; wonderful are Your works, and my soul knows it very well.

Psalm	139:14

My Child,

>When a great artist paints a masterpiece, he knows it. He steps back, and his heart fills with pride and awe at his work. That's what happened when I created you. I stepped back and marveled at my creation. You are beautiful to me. I made you with care and precision and pride.

If you are ever tempted to belittle yourself or feel insecure about your shortcomings, just know that you are perfect in my sight. I am totally pleased with my creation. The world is a better place because you are in it.

When I look at you, I see who you have been, who you are, and who I am making you. It's the total you I marvel at. Begin to see yourself through my eyes, and you will marvel too. You are my perfect work in progress.

The Artist,
>God

== == ==   == == == == == == == == ==

YOU WERE CREATED FOR RELATIONSHIPS

Two are better than one, because they have a good
reward for their toil. For if they fall, one will lift up his
fellow; but woe to him who is alone when he falls and
has not another to lift him up. Again, if two lie together,
they are warm; but how can one be warm alone? And
though a man might prevail against one who is alone, two
will withstand him. A threefold cord is not quickly broken.

| Ecclesiastes | 4:9-12 RSV |

My Son,

>Many men are so focused on their own lives that they don't even
know why they are alive. I didn't create man for the sake of his own
existence. I created him for the relationships that come about as a
result of that existence.

If you are in an intimate friendship with me, you will naturally seek out
deep relationships with others. You won't be content with surface
relationships and small talk. You won't choose to be a lone wolf,
focused solely on your own needs. You will become marvelously
interconnected with others.

But you have to choose deep relationships. You have to reach out to
others and sacrifice to meet people halfway. You have to humble
yourself, listen to others, be sincere, care deeply, and ask forgiveness
when you have damaged a friendship.

Let me into the deep places of your being, my son, and you'll find
yourself more willing to become interconnected.

Your Best Friend,
>God

== == ==   == == == == == == == == ==

STEP OUT OF THE RAIN

**Through two unchangeable things, in which
it is impossible that God should prove false,
we who have fled for refuge might have strong
encouragement to seize the hope set before us.**

Hebrews | 6:18 RSV

My Son,

>Don't ever doubt my ability to hold you and keep you. It is so
important for you to believe in my goodness and the consistency of
my grace toward you. If you doubt it, you won't really understand who
I am or be able to trust your life to me.

I am your shelter from the storms of your life at all times, wherever
those storms may be (in your relationships, in your finances, in your
work, in your worries). The openness of my arms and the safety of my
shelter are constant. But only you can choose to believe this and step
out of the rain.

Son, believe in my goodness and my shelter. Run to me now and feel
the safety of my protection and the security of my presence. Step out
of the rain.

Your Shelter,
>God

== == ==   == == == == == == == == ==

THE WAY OF FORGIVENESS

He who forgives an offense seeks love, but he who repeats a matter alienates a friend.

Proverbs | 17:9 RSV

My Son,

>Whenever somebody does you wrong, it's tempting to hold it over his head and make him feel bad in return. After all, he deserves everything bad that's coming to him. He did you wrong first.

But I am calling you to be a man who forgives. Any wimp can hold a grudge, suck his thumb, and pout. It takes a real man to lay down his pride and honestly forgive someone who's done him wrong. I'm not just talking about telling the other person that you forgive him. I'm talking about really forgiving him in your heart. Don't give him what you think he deserves. Give him what I say he deserves: forgiveness. If you do this, you will feel the weight of unforgiveness lifting off of you, and you'll discover a new freedom to love the one who has wronged you. Walk the way of forgiveness.

The One Who Forgives,
>God

== == ==   == == == == == == == == ==

A NEW SONG EVERY DAY

Give thanks to the Lord with the lyre; sing praises
to Him with a harp of ten strings. Sing to Him
a new song; play skillfully with a shout of joy.

Psalm 33:2-3

My Son,

>Every day that you live, you have a chance to create a beautiful new song for me. Your heart is the voice, your actions are the instrument, and your life that day is the song that you create. When you wake up in the morning, begin to warm up your voice through prayer and worship. And as you step onto the stage of your daily experiences, let the instrument of your actions join your heart's voice in perfect harmony.

Even if you go to work at the same office at the same time every day, each day is still completely unique and filled with the chance for new music. When your eyes are open to each day's beauty, you become free to be creative. Love becomes art, and your life becomes worship.

Son, you are my musician. Your voice and your instrument create melodies that please my heart. Approach each new day as an opportunity for fresh composition.

Your Audience of One,
>God

== == ==   == == == == == == == == ==

BE PATIENT WITH MY VISIONS FOR YOUR LIFE

**Let us not lose heart in doing good, for in
due time we will reap if we do not grow weary.**

Galatians **6:9**

My Son,

>When I give you a word about something I want you to do, it is
important to wait for the right timing.

To use a far-fetched example, if I tell you that I want you to go dive off
the diving board at the local pool, it would be important to wait until
there was water in the pool. Wanting to see visions realized in your
own timing can be like this, and rushing ahead can get you quite a
few bumps on the head, or worse.

I have specific dreams that I have placed in your heart and promises I
have spoken to you. If you feel that they aren't coming true in time,
don't get frustrated and rush up to the diving board. My timing is
perfect, and I can see all the factors that you can't. Trust me, when
the time is right, I'll let you know, and the pool will definitely be full. Be
patient with the visions I give you for your life.

My timing is perfect,
>God

== == ==   == == == == == == == == ==

DON'T GIVE UP ON THE CHURCH

At midnight there was a shout, "Behold, the bridegroom! Come out to meet him."

Matthew 25:6

My Son,

>Many Christians have given up on the Church. They believe in me, but they have lost their faith in the fellowship of believers. Those who give up have usually been hurt by someone in the church. Or they're fed up with "the hypocrisy of organized religion." I don't want you to fall into this spiritual sinkhole.

The Church is the bride of Christ. Jesus is the Bridegroom who's coming back for a spotless and perfected bride. Though she's not perfect or beautiful yet, she is still betrothed to Jesus. And every Christian is called to beautify the bride for the return of her groom.

So, don't give up on the church. You are a part of her and can't truly stand apart. Jesus is not coming back for a scattered group of spiritual know-it-alls who mock his bride. He's coming back for a group of people who choose to accept the church's imperfections as their own responsibility and are committed to perfecting her.

The Bridegroom is coming,
>God

== == ==   == == == == == == == == ==

CHOOSE THE THINGS THAT WILL LAST

Do not store up for yourselves treasures on earth, where moth and rust destroy, and where thieves break in and steal. But store up for yourselves treasures in heaven, where neither moth nor rust destroys, and where thieves do not break in or steal.

Matthew 6:19-20

My Son,

>All the material things you've gathered around yourself won't be going with you to heaven. When your earthly body dies, you'll have to empty the pockets of your life, take off your earthly clothes, and step into eternity. When you do that, you'll see what was really important in life. You'll see the things that are passing away and the things that are lasting.

Relationships, love, salvation, worship, and true peace are eternal and will stay with you. Watches and cars and boats and houses will be left behind. There's nothing wrong with enjoying these things on earth. But maintain a heavenly perspective on what they are—temporary and fading pleasures. Your life on earth is so short, and eternity is so long. Don't invest your life in amassing material things that you will just have to hand over in the end. Choose the things that will last.

The Lord of the Eternal,
>God

== == ==   == == == == == == == == ==

CLEAN THE WAX OUT

**Hear, you deaf! And look, you blind,
that you may see.**

Isaiah 42:18

My Son,

>Have you ever heard someone say, "God told me this or that"? Does it ever make you wonder, *How did he hear God's voice, and why don't I?*

Sometimes I speak through circumstances; occasionally I have to knock you to the ground and speak audibly as I did to Paul on the road to Damascus. But mostly I speak in a still, small voice to your spiritual ears.

There are lots of things that can build up in your spiritual ears. If you're always in a rush, you'll miss the stillness of my voice. If you're seeking to control your own life, you won't be able to hear the subtlety of my voice over your own loud voice of self-rule. If you aren't seeking me daily for direction, your ear won't be tuned in to the tone of my voice.

If you can't hear me, it's time to clean the wax out of your ears. It's time to slow down, be quiet, and listen. When your ears are open, you will hear what I've been saying all along.

The One Who Speaks,
>God

== == ==   == == == == == == == == ==

DAILY DIRECTION

Blessed is the man who listens to me, watching daily at my gates, waiting at my doorposts.

| | Proverbs | 8:34 | |

My Son,

>Do you ever wonder why I don't just explain the rest of your life to you today? Picture your life as a long road trip. If I explained detailed directions for a place I wanted you to go in five years, you wouldn't understand them. That's because those directions would start from where you will be in five years, not from where you are now.

Directions for your life voyage come mainly in the form of daily revelation. That's because I want you to hear, trust, and then move. This step-by-step approach increases your faith and keeps you from trying to run down and tackle the rest of your life in one day.

Because the revelation comes daily, it's important that you get alone with me each morning and receive your directions for that leg of the trip. Come to me, and I will show you the next step to take.

Your Daily Direction,
>God

== == ==   == == == == == == == == ==

DESTROY THE HIGH PLACES

Then you shall drive out all the inhabitants of the land from before you, and destroy all their figured stones, and destroy all their molten images and demolish all their high places.

| | | Numbers | | 33:52 | | | |

My Son,

>Some of the Israelites rebelled and built pagan altars on the high places where they sacrificed to other gods. Each new king of Israel had a choice to either destroy the pagan altars or to let the idolatry continue.

It's tempting to look down on the Israelites for choosing the high places over me. Well, you have your own high places. You have secret altars to things that you have put over me. When you fall away from me, you run to these "gods," thinking that they can meet your needs better than I can. Whether those gods are work, lust, or just laziness, they are still gods that set themselves up against my rule in your life.

Son, just like the kings of the Israelites, you are going to have to choose whether to destroy the high places in your life or whether you will continue to slink off and seek the blessing of gods that are powerless to save you. Destroy the high places, and worship me alone.

The Only One Worthy of Your Worship,
>God

== == ==   == == == == == == == == ==

FORGIVE THEM WHEN THEY DON'T KNOW WHAT THEY'RE DOING

Jesus was saying, "Father, forgive them; for they do not know what they are doing." And they cast lots, dividing up His garments among themselves.

| Luke | 23:34 |

My Son,

>Do you wait to forgive someone until he's good and sorry for what he's done? Does it make you mad when someone does you wrong and can't even see it?

Jesus forgave, even when no one asked him for forgiveness. His compassion was so huge that he even forgave the Roman guards who had nailed him to the cross and mocked him until the end.

Son, don't wait to forgive. There will be times when the person who hurt you will never see it, even if you bring it to his attention. At that point, you need to choose to forgive, rather than carry that resentment around. Jesus could have glared in anger at those guards from the cross, but it wouldn't have hurt anything but his own heart. He wasn't concerned with making them acknowledge their wrong. He was more concerned with their need for heavenly forgiveness. Follow Jesus' example and forgive, even when people don't see their own sinfulness.

Your Father,
>God

FORGIVE, FORGET, AND MOVE ON

As far as the east is from the west, so far has He removed our transgressions from us.

Psalm 103:12 NIV

My Son,

>When I forgive you, I throw that sin out of sight and out of mind. When that happens, you and I have a completely new start. I'm not holding a grudge or saying, "Yeah, I'll forgive you, but I'll be watching for your next mistake, so you'd better watch your step." No, when I forgive, we make a fresh start, and I have new hope for our relationship.

Son, this is the way I want you to forgive the one who hurt you. Don't just forgive, but pray to have his offense completely stricken from the record. Move on in a new hope for your relationship. Forgive the way that I forgive you: forgiving, forgetting, and moving on.

Always Hopeful,
>God

== == ==   == == == == == == == == ==

HELP MY CHILDREN IN NEED

**I was hungry, and you gave Me something to eat;
I was thirsty, and you gave Me something to
drink; I was a stranger, and you invited Me in.**

Matthew   25:35

My Son,

>If your child were in need and someone helped him, wouldn't it bless
you? Wouldn't you feel a special kinship with that person who had
helped?

When people help my children, they bless me. But when people who
are capable of giving things selfishly withhold them from my children,
they withhold those things from me as well. I am so close to the
needy that I can feel how they are being treated.

Son, I am calling you to love the unlovable, not in theory but in action.
When you are presented with opportunities to help someone in need,
jump in there and do it. When you do, you will not only be blessing
the ones who need help, but their Father in Heaven as well.

Father to the Needy and Those Who Love Them,
>God

== == ==   == == == == == == == == ==

HERE TODAY (YOUR DAILY BURDENS)

**Blessed be the Lord, who daily bears
our burden, the God who is our salvation.**

| Psalm | | 68:19 | |

My Son,

>I didn't just give you a two thousand-year-old gift of salvation, tied up with a nice bow, and then disappear, leaving you to bear your day-to-day burdens on your own. I did give you salvation when I sent my Son to bear your burdens and your sin at the cross, but it wasn't meant to be a static gift. I gave you the gift that keeps on giving. You see, I am still here bearing your burdens every day. I love you so much that I care about what you care about, and I am hurt by what hurts you.

I know the burdens you are carrying today. Don't just picture Jesus on the cross in Jerusalem two thousand years ago. Picture him by your side right now, today, helping you carry your daily load. I'm right beside you.

Your Present-tense Savior,
>God

== == ==   == == == == == == == == ==

HUDDLE UP

**When they were alone,
He expounded all things to His disciples.**

| 🖨 📎 ✝ 🤍 ▼ | Mark | 4:34 NKJV ▼ | ✉ ✌ 📖 📋 |

My Son,

>I always want to let the people on my team know the game plan. One way to look at a prayer meeting is as a football huddle. All my players are regrouping after a tough play. They are sharing their concerns with me and talking about the strategy of the opponent. I am the quarterback and the coach. I stand in the huddle and give direction, affirmation, and challenge. We establish our game plan, and our "amen" is like the "break" at the end of the huddle. Then we go out and execute our individual assignments, and we work as a team. If we all carry out the plan, our opponent is bound to be soundly defeated.

Son, have you felt lacking in direction and strategy in your spiritual walk? There's no need to drift out there alone. Come together with me and your teammates, and let's get back on track. Huddle up.

Your Coach,
>God

== == ==   == == == == == == == == ==

THE REFRIGERATOR AND THE BIBLE

Ho! Every one who thirsts, come to the waters; and you who have no money come, buy and eat. Come, buy wine and milk without money and without cost. Why do you spend money for what is not bread, and your wages for what does not satisfy? Listen carefully to Me, and eat what is good, and delight yourself in abundance.

Isaiah 55:1-2

My Son,

>Next time you go to your refrigerator to get something to eat, I want you to think about the Bible. That's right, think about the Bible. If you're physically hungry, your hunger always takes you to the refrigerator because that's where the food is. Well, the Bible is where the spiritual food is kept. So when you are spiritually hungry, that's where you should go!

My words in the Bible have a supernatural way of nourishing the spiritual part of you, the part that loves me and my ways more than anything. If you feel as if you don't love me more than anything else and you don't feel close to me, you are definitely spiritually hungry. If you feel as if you aren't really loving the people around you, you need spiritual food.

Let your spiritual hunger send you to the Bible to be spiritually fed. As you read, know that every word is feeding your spirit and helping it grow.

Come and get it,
>God

== == ==   == == == == == == == == ==

I CHOOSE YOU

When the Pharisees saw this, they said to His disciples, "Why is your Teacher eating with the tax collectors and sinners?" But when Jesus heard this, He said, "It is not those who are healthy who need a physician, but those who are sick."

Matthew   9:11–12

My Son,

>Do you remember those pre-game scenes of standing in a group of boys waiting as the captains chose people one by one? They always chose the fastest and the strongest first. After a while, all the boys were picked, until there was that last, smaller, slower, weaker kid—the kid that no one wanted. Sheepishly, he hung his head as one of the captains reluctantly said, "All right, I guess I'll take him."

When Jesus came to earth, he changed this type of scene forever. He was the team captain who came for that weak kid. He looked at him and saw the perfect athlete. Jesus stood and picked his whole team in reverse order. He chose a tax collector for a disciple and a prostitute for a friend. He ate with the unholy and embraced the unclean. He wanted everyone, but his heart spoke up for the needy first.

Never again do you have to stand ashamed as the others get picked. Jesus turned the system upside down.

The One Who Chooses You,
>God

== == ==   == == == == == == == == ==

I WILL CHANGE YOUR NAME

The nations will see your righteousness, and all kings your glory; and you will be called by a new name which the mouth of the LORD will designate.

Isaiah	62:2

My Son,

>Many times boys grow up with fathers who curse them rather than bless them, who speak critical names over them rather than positive ones. These boys will carry those negative names into manhood, haunted by names like "Failure," "Stupid," or "Crybaby."

Son, I am your loving Father. If your earthly father has done this to you, I want to change your name. If you have ever believed that your name was "Worthless" or "Insignificant" or "Rebel" or "Black Sheep," I want your new name to be "Priceless in My Sight," "Awesome Child of the Father," "Eternally Loved and Accepted."

With me in your life, you don't have to be haunted and driven by the old negative names. Now the old has gone, and the new has come. Let me change not only your name, but your destiny.

The One Who Knows Who You Really Are,
>God

== == ==   == == == == == == == == ==

I'M NEVER DONE WITH YOU

> She said, "Who would have said to Abraham that Sarah would nurse children? Yet I have borne him a son in his old age."

Genesis **21:7**

My Son,

>I'm never finished with you. Even if you believe that you're dried up, washed out, and irrelevant, you're not. Anyone who is mine has the constant hope of new beginnings.

I will accomplish the purposes I have for you on the earth. As long as you are alive and living for me, you are standing in the perfect place to be used to accomplish amazing things for me. Don't let the world set deadlines for your ability to accomplish things. It's never too late to go back to school, to get a new job, to start a new ministry, to get into shape, or to do whatever it is I am calling you to do.

If you are listening and watching for my purposes in your life, you are always in your prime. So go for it, son! I will never be finished with you.

The Author of the Next Chapter,
>God

== == ==   == == == == == == == == ==

LET IT GO

The Lord's lovingkindnesses indeed never cease,
for His compassions never fail. They are new
every morning; great is Your faithfulness.

Lamentations   3:22-23

My Son,

>Sometimes you make mistakes that are unchangeable. Once you do mess up, it doesn't help to beat yourself up about it. Unless you're able to build a time machine and go back to correct the problem, the best thing you can do is accept it and move on.

The truth is, you take a lot longer to forgive yourself than I take to forgive you. This is because I know how to let things in the past stay in the past. There are three key elements to self-forgiveness. The first is to ask for and receive my forgiveness. The second is to pray for the peace to accept what you can't change. The third is to pray for the strength to change what you can change.

Then you can let yourself off of the hook, knowing that I've forgiven you and that you've done your best to pick up the pieces. So don't be harder on yourself than I am. Receive power from me to let go of any old guilt and move on.

The Ever-forgiving One,
>God

== == ==   == == == == == == == == ==

BE HONEST ABOUT YOUR PAIN

He heals the brokenhearted and binds up their wounds.

| Psalm | 147:3 |

My Son,

>If someone has a broken arm, he goes to the doctor to have it set and put in a cast. He makes that visit to the doctor count, because he wants his arm to be straight and right.

Mankind has a brokenness—a soul-sickness. But what many people do is come to my office on Sunday and act as if nothing's broken. The conversation goes something like this.

"So what seems to be the trouble?"
"Oh, nothing Doc, I'm doing fine."
"But your X-ray shows a massive fracture of your left arm."
"Oh, no, nothing wrong with me. By the way, did you see how nicely dressed I am?"
"Yes, but I don't understand. Why did you come to the doctor if you aren't willing to let me fix what's broken?"

Son, you have a soul-sickness just as everyone else does. I already know what's going on. I've seen the X-ray. So don't pretend. Cry out to me. I want to heal you. And don't forget, I also make house calls.

Your Healer,
>God

== == ==   == == == == == == == == ==

LIVING IN A STATE OF LOVED-NESS

**He predestined us to adoption as sons through Jesus Christ
to Himself, according to the kind intention of His will, to
the praise of the glory of His grace, which He freely bestowed
on us in the Beloved. In Him we have redemption through
His blood, the forgiveness of our trespasses, according
to the riches of His grace which He lavished on us.**

Ephesians | 1:5-8

My Son,

>Being loved is not just an act. It's a state of being. If you needed
your wife to follow you everywhere, constantly saying, "I love you,"
you wouldn't be living in that state of being. Being loved is not
needing constant proof. It is knowing the love of the one who loves
you and then living in a state of loved-ness.

The tragedy on earth is that it's so hard to trust in human love. People
let you down, and you end up finding it hard to hope in unconditional
love. So you reach out for "reassure me" human love.

Son, I want you to let me heal you of all the times you were loved and
then let down. I want to help you trust in love again. I want you to
know my unconditional, nonstop, full-power love. If you believe that I
love you, you can live in the reality of my love at all times and never
have to rely on "reassure me" love again.

Your Place of Loved-ness,
>God

== == ==   == == == == == == == == ==

LOVE ALWAYS HAS A CHOICE

Choose life in order that you may live, you and your descendants, by loving the LORD your God, by obeying His voice, and by holding fast to Him.

Deuteronomy | 30:19-20

My Son,

>Suppose when you met the woman you wanted to marry, you had the option to give her a potion that would make her fall madly in love with you? Would you give it to her? If you did, you'd always wonder whether she would have loved you for yourself.

Forced love isn't real love. Real love always has the ability to choose. A beautiful thing about marriage is knowing that, out of all the other guys out there, this woman chose you to spend the rest of her life with.

Son, I created you to be in an intimate, personal relationship with me. But I didn't create you with puppet strings so I could dance you around, singing, "I love God, I love God!" I gave you a will to choose me or to choose to turn your back on me. I love you so much, and I am waiting for you to choose me over the things that lead you away from me.

The One Who Chose You First,
>God

== == ==   == == == == == == == == ==

LOVE BEYOND ALL REASON

As high as the heavens are above the earth, so great
is His lovingkindness toward those who fear Him.

Psalm 103:11

My Son,

>There is no device created that can measure my love for you. My
love will always cease to make human sense at some point because
it isn't meant to be measured in human terms.

I love you outside the lines, over the top, beyond the extreme. When
you think I'm bound to stop loving you, I have only just begun to love
you. I love way beyond 100 percent, and I don't hold anything back.

Trying to measure my mercy and compassion is like trying to gauge
an emotion with a calculator. No equation will ever do my love justice.
Expect more of my love than you've ever expected. Don't try to
reason it out. Just open your heart to it.

Unlimited Love,
>God

== == ==   == == == == == == == == ==

DON'T STOP IN THE MIDDLE

I am confident of this very thing, that He who began a good work in you will perfect it until the day of Christ Jesus.

| Philippians | 1:6 |

My Son,

>Have you ever reorganized a closet in your house? You have to pull everything out before you can set it all back in the right place. If someone were to come over in the middle of the process and see what you were doing, he might say, "What a mess! You must not care about your house." But that wouldn't be the truth at all. Even though it may look as if a bomb exploded, you'd know you were putting your house in order.

Sometimes your life seems like that closet. I have begun to rearrange everything for your benefit. But I know it's tempting to stop me in the middle and say, "Wait a minute, everything wasn't so bad before. At least all my spiritual closet clutter was tucked away, and I didn't have to look at it." But if you try to stop in the middle, you will never know the blessing of having your life completely set in order. Allow me to finish the job, my son. It may feel like a mess now, but it will be perfectly arranged in the end.

Setting You Straight,
>God

== == ==   == == == == == == == == ==

NEW WINESKINS

No one puts new wine into old wineskins;
otherwise the new wine will burst the skins and
it will be spilled out, and the skins will be ruined.
But new wine must be put into fresh wineskins.

Luke | 5:37-38

My Son,

>Before I revealed my love to you, you were filled with the wine of your own self-importance and selfishness. When you were convicted by my truth, I began to empty you of that old, selfish brand of wine.

But you are still not ready to receive the potent new wine I want to pour into you. Your old perceptions of who I am and how I love and act are an unsuitable container for my truth. Emptying the old stuff isn't enough. Before you can be filled with the new Spirit, you need to let me transform the whole container. Let me renew your mind and make it ready to receive the wine of my new life.

The Giver of New Wine,
>God

== == ==   == == == == == == == == ==

PICK UP THE PHONE

There is a friend who sticks closer than a brother.

| | Proverbs | 18:24 NIV | |

My Son,

>If our relationship were like a phone conversation, your choosing to sin would be like choosing to hang up on me. But though you might hang up, I'd stay by the phone. Your sin can't run me off that easily. I'd be right here waiting for you to pick up the phone and resume our conversation.

If you've sinned, you may feel as if you're a million miles away from me—as if you've moved outside of my area code—but that's a wrong perception. Guilt creates that false sense of distance. The truth is, I haven't moved. I'm still right here. All you need to do is earnestly repent and reach for the phone. You will find me patiently waiting on the other end of the line—waiting to forgive you and take up where we left off.

The One Who's Always Here,
>God

== == ==   == == == == == == == == ==

PRAY WITH HUMBLE CONFIDENCE

**The Pharisee stood and was praying this to himself:
"God, I thank You that I am not like other people:
swindlers, unjust, adulterers, or even like this tax collector."**

Luke 18:11

My Son,

>Prayer is the language of the humble, not the self-righteous. When you truly understand what I have made possible to you through the suffering of Christ, then you will understand how to pray. But when you pray, trusting in your own righteousness as compared to other people's, you are so clueless. Anyone who prays like that is like a garbage man saying, "I was the cleanest garbage man at the end of the workday." It's laughable.

Only through the cleansing blood of Jesus are you able to stand in my presence and pray. And this cleansing is made available to the dirtiest garbage man as well as to the most immaculately groomed CEO, because both need it.

Son, I encourage you to come to me with humble confidence, being humbled by the knowledge of my grace and confident in the holiness of Christ.

The One Who Hears the Humble,
>God

== == ==   == == == == == == == == ==

PROGRESS, NOT PERFECTION

The good that I want, I do not do, but I practice the very evil that I do not want. But if I am doing the very thing I do not want, I am no longer the one doing it, but sin which dwells in me.

| Romans | 7:19-20 |

Son,

>Has anyone ever called you a hypocrite for believing in me but not acting perfect all the time? Here is a news flash. You are a hypocrite. Any human who stands up strongly for something is immediately in danger of being a hypocrite and will eventually become one. Why? Because humans aren't perfect. That's why they aren't able to walk out their convictions perfectly.

But Christianity is not about having the perfect spiritual journey. It's about knowing which direction to take and doing your best to get there. Don't buy into the need to prove all the cynics wrong about your hypocrisy. There is freedom in accepting your imperfection, trusting my guidance, and continuing to move forward with me.

The Lover of Hypocrites,
>God

== == ==   == == == == == == == == ==

RECEIVE IT LIKE A CHILD

**Truly I say to you, whoever does not receive the
kingdom of God like a child will not enter it at all.**

Mark   10:15

My Son,

>When a young boy goes into a huge amusement park, he is in
absolute awe of what he sees. He delights in the sights, the sounds,
and the feel of the experience he's being given. He doesn't question
how things work or how much it all costs. He just takes it all in.

Son, receive my love like a child. Receive it as if every wonderful
thing you have ever imagined has come to life. Instead of wondering
how I could love you in the midst of your sin, just receive that I do.
Instead of wondering how eternity can exist, just walk into that eternal
light. Instead of doubting that I could really heal you and make you
whole, receive the miracle of my healing.

Unlike an amusement park, the kingdom of Heaven is not based on
make-believe. It's based on the deepest reality you have ever known.
Walk into it with wonder.

The One Who Loves You,
>God

== == ==   == == == == == == == == ==

RETURN TO EDEN

I remember the days of old; I meditate on all Your doings;
I muse on the work of Your hands. I stretch out my hands
to You; my soul longs for You, as a parched land.

Psalm | 143:5-6

My Son,

>There is a part of every man that is homesick for the Garden of
Eden. That's because I created man for the Garden, not for the fallen
world. But man rejected a perfect relationship with me because he
didn't want to submit to my will. Instead, he chose to break that
relationship and walk into the fallen world of self-rule.

Since I created you for the Garden and not the world around you, you
can feel the separation deep down in your heart. You know that you
were created for more. You feel the emptiness of worldly things, and
you long for resolution to the disharmony of your soul.

Son, Jesus Christ is the gateway to Eden. He is the return trip to an
unbroken relationship with me. In him, you can have true peace,
because you will finally be living where I created you to live. Eden is
not a place anymore; it is a relationship. If you feel homesick in your
soul, come to Christ and return to Eden.

I'll be waiting,
>God

== == ==   == == == == == == == == ==

SUNTANS AND PEELING

If we walk in the Light as He Himself is in the Light, we have fellowship with one another, and the blood of Jesus His Son cleanses us from all sin.

1 John   1:7

My Son,

>Have you ever worked really hard in the summer to get a good suntan? You spend hours in the sun, putting on suntan lotion to achieve the bronze look you want. But at the end of the summer when the weather changes, it's hard to keep up the schedule. Your skin cracks and peels, and the suntan fades.

There are many people who spend their spiritual lives going from summer tans to winter fades and back to summer tans. They have a bright spiritual experience when they lay out in my presence and coat their spirits with my Word and the anointing oil of my Holy Spirit. But when the season changes and they experience the winter of trial, their suntans begin to crack in ugly lines of compromise.

A powerful Christian walk is not a pumped-up, sunny-weekend experience. It is a daily walk in the sun. It is being willing to stand spiritually vulnerable before me and absorb all I have for you. Seek me daily to keep your spiritual tan.

The Father of Light,
>God

THE SERVANT'S STRENGTH

Whoever wishes to become great among you shall be your servant, and whoever wishes to be first among you shall be your slave.

| Matthew | 20:26-27 |

My Son,

>In the legends of King Arthur, whoever could remove the sword Excalibur from the stone where it had been placed would inherit the kingdom. The strongest and bravest men pulled, postured, and sweated, but the sword wouldn't budge. Then Arthur, a little boy squire in need of a sword for the knight he served, drew Excalibur easily from the stone in his moment of need. With that act of servitude, he unknowingly became king.

Those who know they are weak are humble, and that humility can empower them with the incredible strength to serve. A servant will always inherit the kingdom of heaven. Even though he may be lowly, he has the power to be lifted up. Son, I want you to have the strength of servanthood. Don't seek to take my kingdom by force. Just seek to serve me and others, and you will inherit it in the process.

Your Servant King,
>God

== == ==   == == == == == == == == ==

YOUR DAILY BREAD

Give us this day our daily bread.

Matthew 6:11

My Son,

>I have created your body to need refueling. Without replenishing supplies of food and water, you will die. Your lungs also need constant filling. You can't just take one deep breath and have all the oxygen you need for the rest of your life.

In the same way, I didn't fill you with my Spirit once only, and that was that. You need continuous spiritual refueling too. Seek me daily for the nourishment you need. I want to feed your spirit life-giving food. I want you to breathe in my Holy Spirit with every breath so that it can give you the strength you need to live your faith actively and powerfully. Seek me and receive the daily bread I have for you, my son.

Your Provider,
>God

== == ==   == == == == == == == == ==

THE FEAR OF THE LORD

In the fear of the Lord there is strong confidence,
and his children will have refuge. The fear of the Lord is
a fountain of life, that one may avoid the snares of death.

Proverbs 14:26-27

My Child,

>I don't want you to be afraid of me, but I do want you to have a healthy respect for me. I don't want you to spend your life trembling in terror of my presence, but I do want you to have the wisdom to stay close to my shelter and strength.

A man who has taken hold of a rock in the middle of a roaring river isn't afraid of the rock. But he does have a healthy fear of letting go of that rock. That's an intelligent kind of fear—one that has found its source of confidence and is afraid of letting go.

You have found your stability in me. Don't fear me. Instead, stand in awe of me and maintain a healthy fear of letting go and being swept away by the rapids from which I've saved you.

Your Confidence,
>God

== == ==   == == == == == == == == ==

THE GIFT OF YOURSELF

Peter said, "I do not possess silver and gold, but what I do have I give to you: In the name of Jesus Christ the Nazarene—walk!"

| Acts | 3:6 |

My Son,

>When many people think of giving to the church or to the work of the gospel, they think about handing over some money. But that is only part of what giving is about. When I sent the disciples out on the first Christian "mission trip," all they had was the power and grace I had given them. They didn't have money to give, but by showing up and reaching out, they gave the most important gift of all.

Son, the most important gift you have to give to the work of my gospel is yourself. Sending money to good causes is respectable and needed, but placing yourself in my hands is incredible. Don't rob yourself of the blessing of letting me use you to touch someone else's life with my salvation and healing. I want you to experience the exciting adventures that we'll share when you give me the gift of yourself.

Let's go,
>God

== == ==   == == == == == == == == ==

THE OCEAN AND THE BATHTUB

All have sinned and fall short of the glory of God.

Romans 3:23 NIV

My Son,

>Do you know that it is as possible for someone to drown in his own bathtub as it is for him to drown in the Pacific Ocean? Being self-righteous can be a little bit like drowning in a bathtub. The man who prides himself on being good and moral thumbs his nose at an openly immoral man who is drowning in an ocean of obvious and public sin. But the prideful, judgmental man is actually drowning in a bathtub of self-righteousness.

Every man is imperfect and has fallen short of my perfection. Because of this, it doesn't matter whether he drowns a hundred miles down or an inch below the surface. He's just as dead spiritually. Only through Jesus' going down to the depths and being raised up above the surface can anyone be saved. So, my son, if you're tempted to judge others, remember that the only reason your head is above water is that my grace holds you there. I didn't rescue you from the depths just to have you drown in a bathtub of self-righteousness.

Your Rescuer,
>God

== == ==   == == == == == == == == ==

THE SPEED OF GRACE

**Therefore let us draw near with confidence
to the throne of grace, so that we may receive
mercy and find grace to help in time of need.**

Hebrews   4:16

My Son,

>On the Internet, it doesn't matter how fast a site's server can pump out information. If the person visiting that site has a slow connection to the Web, then he will receive the information slowly. I pump out love at one speed—unconditionally, full throttle, all the time. But some people are incapable of receiving unconditional love. Their connection with me may be slowed by their own low self-esteem or a faulty concept of the way I love. Consequently, they can only receive love at the conditional level. That leaves them starved for the "data" they need to grow spiritually.

Son, if you are unable to receive the totality of my love because of a slow connection, then it's time to upgrade your modem. With the speed of a new grace connection, you will begin to get a clear picture of my love. Connect to me at the speed of grace.

Your Server,
>God

== == ==   == == == == == == == == ==

THE STRENGTH OF NEEDING ME

Behold, God is my salvation, I will trust and
not be afraid; for the LORD God is my strength
and song, and He has become my salvation.

| Isaiah | 12:2 |

My Son,

>Some people think that needing me is a sign of weakness. They
couldn't be further from the truth.

You probably know men who never ask for help. These men usually
get a lot accomplished but end up tired and stressed all the time.
Even if they meet the deadline, they don't get to share the joy of the
success with anyone else. And they're so burned out that the next
project threatens to get the best of them.

The strongest man in the world is the man who has others to hold him up
and help him. He gets stronger with each project, because he has the
help he needs. He also experiences the camaraderie of the team and
has the peace of knowing he can count on team support in the future.
When you became humble enough to ask for my help, that was when
you became strong. Continue to be weak enough to ask for my strength.

Your Strength,
>God

== == ==   == == == == == == == == ==

THE WOUND OF UNFORGIVENESS

Therefore if you are presenting your offering at the altar, and there remember that your brother has something against you, leave your offering there before the altar and go; first be reconciled to your brother, and then come and present your offering.

Matthew 5:23-24

My Son,

>Whenever you harbor unforgiveness in your heart, you think you're getting back at the person who harmed you, but you're really just hurting yourself.

If someone stuck a knife in your side, you wouldn't sit there and twist it in deeper to punish your attacker. Of course not. You would pull out the knife as quickly as possible.

The same is true when someone does anything to hurt you. Why would you want to hold on to that pain through unforgiveness? You are the only one who is suffering by holding on to it. Son, go to the people who have harmed you and forgive them. Or if you can't go to them for some reason, come to me and let's take that knife out together through prayer. Don't hold on to unforgiveness. It only hurts you, and that hurts me.

Your Father,
>God

== == ==   == == == == == == == == ==

TRUE FRIEND

There are friends who pretend to be friends.

Proverbs 18:24 RSV

My Son,

>People don't exist merely to meet your needs. If you have friendships that you keep up simply to serve your interests, it's time to reevaluate those friendships. But more importantly, it's time to reevaluate your heart.

A true friend is willing to lay down his life for his friends. He serves them. He sticks by them, even when it gets hard. He doesn't abandon them when they cease to serve his needs. A true friend counts the cost of friendship and pays the price.

Son, I am calling you to be a true friend to the people in your life. I know that you have a limited amount of time and energy. I know you are only human. But I want you to reflect your love for me in the way that you love your friends. I am the friend who sticks closer than a brother, and I want you to be that kind of friend for your friends too.

Your True Friend,
>God

== == ==   == == == == == == == == ==

WALK THROUGH THE DOOR OF MY ACCEPTANCE

The LORD is the portion of my inheritance and my cup;
You support my lot. The lines have fallen to me in
pleasant places; indeed, my heritage is beautiful to me.

Psalm   16:5-6

My Son,

>What if you were the heir to a great fortune and your father was holding a huge banquet in your honor? At the banquet, he was planning to give you your inheritance early. All the tables were set. Delicious food had been shipped in from all over the world. Your father was waiting proudly for you to walk through the door. Would you sit at the gates of your father's house and not enter because you felt as if your father didn't love you enough?

Sadly, this is true of many of my sons. They sit at the gates of the richest inheritance that they will ever receive thinking I don't love them. They believe the lie that I am just here to keep track of their sins and make them pay in the end.

Son, everything is set. The guests have arrived. And I am proudly waiting for you to walk through that door of my unconditional acceptance of you. You are my son in whom I am well pleased. Enter in.

The One Who Accepts You Unconditionally,
>God

== == ==   == == == == == == == == ==

WEAKNESS INTO STRENGTH

Therefore I am well content with weaknesses, with insults, with distresses, with persecutions, with difficulties, for Christ's sake; for when I am weak, then I am strong.

2 Corinthians   12:10

My Child,

>Remember the story of the ugly duckling? He was a swan born by accident into a duck family. He grew up feeling sad and incredibly different. But it was that very difference that eventually matured him into a beautiful adult swan.

Sometimes the characteristic or weakness that you have hated about yourself can become the very thing that ends up blessing you the most. In our relationship, that's true of all of your weaknesses. That's because your weaknesses make you cry out for my strength. When you do cry out in your weakness, that weakness becomes a blessing rather than a curse. It is the very thing that leads you into my arms.

So glory in your weaknesses. Let them lead you to my strength.

Your Strength,
>God

== == ==   == == == == == == == == ==

WHO IS WILLING TO GO?

Then I heard the voice of the Lord, saying,
"Whom shall I send, and who will go for Us?"
Then I said, "Here am I. Send me!"

Isaiah **6:8**

My Son,

>The person I usually choose to use is the guy who shows up and says, "Here I am, Lord. Use me." He doesn't have to be the smartest or the most gifted; he just has to be willing. Isaiah overheard a call that I was making to all of mankind, not specifically to him. He was just tuned in enough to hear it and willing enough to answer it. As a result, I used him to do amazing things for me on the earth.

My call still goes out to all the earth: "Whom will I send and who will go for me?" If you hear it, don't worry about whether you are Mr. Super-Christian or not. Just say, "Here I am Lord. Use me." And I will surely use you to do amazing things. I will fill your mouth with words of truth and gift your hands to do my work. If you are willing, I will send you.

The One Who Seeks a Willing Heart,
>God

== == == == == == == == == == == ==

YOU CAN'T EARN MY LOVE

What I am saying is this: the Law, which came
four hundred and thirty years later, does not
invalidate a covenant previously ratified by God,
so as to nullify the promise. For if the inheritance is
based on law, it is no longer based on a promise; but
God has granted it to Abraham by means of a promise.

| Galatians | 3:17–18 |

My Son,

>If your family owned a huge corporation, you wouldn't go into business headquarters every day and vacuum and mop, hoping to get some sort of paycheck. You would know your own sense of entitlement, security, and acceptance within that company.

Unfortunately, there are children of mine who already have full inheritance of my kingdom, but they still feel a need to earn their place in the company. They're still running the vacuum and mopping up, trying to earn what is already theirs.

Son, your good deeds shouldn't be done to earn my acceptance. They should be done in order to bless others. The spiritual principles that you apply to your life should be applied in order to bless and mature yourself. You already have all of my love. Receive your place in my corporation. I love you as you are—totally.

Your Father,
>God

YOU DON'T HAVE TO CLEAN UP TO COME HOME

God demonstrates His own love toward us, in that while we were yet sinners, Christ died for us.

| Romans | 5:8 |

My Son,

>What if your son ran away and you searched high and low for him? You dreamed about him at night and prayed every day for his return. One day, finally, you see him coming down your driveway, beat-up and dirty.

Would you say to him, "I'm sorry son, it's good to see you and all, but I kind of expected a cleaner son to come home. You'll have to go take a shower and give your wounds some time to heal, and get a job so you can buy some new clothes. Then maybe you can come home"? No way! You'd run and embrace him and weep tears of joy. You'd run a bath for him and nurse him back to health. In the same way, you don't have to clean up before you come to me.

You are my son. No amount of dirt can keep you from my embrace. No wound is too deep for my healing. Come as you are.

Your Father,
>God

== == ==   == == == == == == == == ==

A SURE FOUNDATION

The rain fell, and the floods came, and the winds blew and slammed against that house; and yet it did not fall, for it had been founded on the rock.

| Matthew | 7:25 |

My Son,

>I have provided wonderful spiritual materials and wisdom in my Word for the building of your spiritual house. But there's no sense starting to build until you purchase property on the unshakable rock of my divinity. If you don't believe the truth about the divinity and the death and resurrection of Jesus, then no matter what spiritual principles you glean from my teachings, you will still be ungrounded and shaky.

Plenty of people think Jesus was a good man, a smart teacher, and a prophet. But Jesus was more. He laid himself down to be the ultimate foundation on which to build your life. If you don't start with that solid base, then it doesn't matter what kind of spiritual house you construct; it won't stand in the storms of life. Son, purchase your property on the rock of my Son. When he's your foundation, your house will stand.

Your Foundation,
>God

== == ==   == == == == == == == == ==

DON'T JUST WAIT FOR THEM TO COME

He said to them, "Go into all the world and preach the gospel to all creation."

Mark 16:15

My Son,

>My model for ministry isn't simply "Build it, and they will come." I didn't ask the disciples to build a church after Pentecost and put on culturally relevant programs in hopes that people would come and be saved. I sent them out into the world to seek and save the lost. In the same way, I am not calling you to compartmentalize your Christianity. Instead, I want you to integrate your faith into every aspect of your life. I don't want you to wait to invite friends to church where your pastor will hopefully speak the truth to them for you. Although that can be effective, don't let that be the extent of your outreach.

Look at every area of your life as a mission field. Have a heart of compassion for the needs of those around you and a heart of love that humbly reaches out. Don't just wait for them to come. Go out into all the earth, specifically the places where I've already placed you.

The One Who Sends You,
>God

== == ==   == == == == == == == == ==

DON'T WHITE-KNUCKLE IT

He will arise and shepherd His flock in
the strength of the LORD, in the majesty
of the name of the LORD His God.

| Micah | 5:4 |

My Son,

>Every man is called to be a minister of my Gospel. But I don't want
you to become a white-knuckled minister. White-knuckled ministers
tell people about me because they're supposed to, not because they
want to. Their outreach is based on a commission, not on
compassion. They seek to save the lost but forget to love the
unlovable. They count heads but neglect to heal hearts. Their
knuckles are always white because they are trying to squeeze out a
"respectable" ministry result in their own strength.

Son, don't ever let people become numbers and reaching out become
a duty rather than a joy. Don't see those who come to me as notches
on your spiritual belt. Love them with my love, and it will become a
natural instinct to minister to them. Only my heart of compassion can
release you from your white-knuckled motives for ministry.

The One Who's Called You to Reach Out in My Strength,
>God

== == ==   == == == == == == == == ==

I AM FOR YOU

What then shall we say to these things?
If God is for us, who is against us?

| | | Romans | | 8:31 | | | |

My Son,

>I am not some big, heavenly sheriff, just waiting for you to do something wrong so I can blast you with my condemnation gun. I am more like a father watching you at your best event, cheering you on. I love you, son. I have hopes for your success and plans to guard against your failure. When you are doing the best you can and it just doesn't seem to be good enough, I understand. If you win the game, I rejoice with you. If you lose the game, I am the father who takes you out afterwards to talk about it over a milkshake.

Son, trust in the fact that I am pulling for you, not waiting to pounce on your mistakes. I'm setting you free to do your best—to succeed without any fear of failure. Go for it!

Your Father,
>God

== == ==   == == == == == == == == ==

HAND ME THE GUN

**Therefore I love Your commandments
above gold, yes, above fine gold.**

| | | Psalm | 119:127 | | |

My Son,

>To a child, a handgun might seem like a pretty neat play toy. It's shiny and exciting and makes loud "boom" noises. But a father would never give his young son a handgun to play with, because that father would know the deadly potential of the weapon.

There are certain play toys I have set restrictions on for my children's sake. I have plainly outlined them in my Word and in the Ten Commandments. I am not a killjoy, out to steal your fun. I am setting up a way of living that allows you joy without injury.

Please don't be tantalized by the flashiness of adultery and lust or the exciting lure of worshipping other gods. Don't be tempted by the toys of selfishness. I am your loving father. Hand me the gun.

The One Who Protects You,
>God

== == ==   == == == == == == == == ==

INVESTING WISELY

By wisdom a house is built, and by understanding it is established; and by knowledge the rooms are filled with all precious and pleasant riches.

| Proverbs | 24:3-4 |

My Son,

>The world esteems a man who has a large sum of money in his bank account. They marvel at his ability to draw on that money when he needs it. But what they didn't see all along were the small deposits and wise investments he made over the years that grew his account into its formidable size.

The man of faith is like the man with the large bank account. He makes steady deposits of prayer, thanksgiving, and time with me over the years. He invests himself in things that will bear fruit for my kingdom. And then when it comes time to draw on his account, he has unlimited funds. He has an abundance of blessings to spread around. I have given you spiritual riches, but you have to choose what you will do with them. Invest them wisely, my son.

Your Master,
>God

== == ==   == == == == == == == == ==

MAKE A WAY FOR THE KING

**As it is written in Isaiah the prophet:
"Behold, I send my messenger ahead
of you, who will prepare your way."**

| Mark | | 1:2 | |

My Son,

>In ancient times, before the invention of interstates and superhighways,
traveling was very rough business. There were potholes and rocks,
sandy desert places and thick forests. It was hard for one horse-drawn
cart to navigate and travel, but it was even more demanding for the
king's huge train of vehicles to travel through the land. So before the
king would start on his journey, the call would go out to prepare the way
for the king. Months in advance of the journey, the people would obtain
the king's travel plans. They would begin to remove rocks from the road,
to fill in the valleys, and to make a way through the mountains. They
would go to any length to make a way for the king.

Son, I am your King, and I am moving in your land. I am going out to
bring my people back home to me. Will you find out where I am
moving? Will you make the way free of any obstacles? The call is
going out. Make a way for the King.

On the Move,
>God

== == ==   == == == == == == == == ==

MOVE INTO THE NEIGHBORHOOD

**For God so loved the world, that He gave
His only begotten Son, that whoever believes
in Him shall not perish, but have eternal life.**

John   3:16

My Son,

>When Jesus wanted to minister to the human family, he moved into
the neighborhood. He didn't just yell down from Heaven, "Get your act
together, or else!" He entered into their jumbled existence and began
to help them straighten it all out. He understood their struggles, and
he had compassion for their pain. He cared for more than their eternal
souls. He cared about every single aspect of human life.

Son, I want you to establish lifelong relationships with the people you
minister to. I want you to move into the neighborhood of their worries,
joys, hopes, and dreams. Don't have only my heart for the salvation
of mankind. Also have my heart for the welfare of the individual men
and women I've placed in your life. Don't just hand out spiritual
literature. Invest yourself in people's lives.

The One Who Lives It Out with You,
>God

== == ==   == == == == == == == == ==

NO ONE WINS THE RAT RACE

**I press on toward the goal for the prize
of the upward call of God in Christ Jesus.**

| | | | | | | **Philippians** | | **3:14** | | | | | |

My Son,

>The society you live in is obsessed with busyness. The lie of the rat race is that the one who accomplishes the most, works the hardest, and dies with the most toys, wins in the end. This is a fatally flawed perspective based on what you do rather than who you are.

I am more interested in who you are becoming than what you're doing. You could spend all of your energy chasing down the things of this world and never reach a meaningful destination. You don't want to cross the finish line only to have the prize fall apart in your hands.

I encourage you to pull out of the rat race and spend your energy on what is worthwhile. Spend your time wisely, seeking me and my purposes. I will guide you and give you the strength to press on toward the goal that is in Christ Jesus. His is the only race worth running.

The Way Out of the Rat Race,
>God

== == ==   == == == == == == == == ==

RACE CARS AND STATION WAGONS

When they blew 300 trumpets, the Lord set the sword
of one against another even throughout the whole army;
and the army fled as far as Beth-shittah toward Zererah,
as far as the edge of Abel-meholah, by Tabbath.

Judges 7:22

My Son,

>If a high performance race car won the Indianapolis 500, it would just be a headline in the next day's paper. But if a mother's standard car-pool station wagon won the race, it would be given a page in "Ripley's Believe It or Not."

In many ways I have created you like the high-performance race car, and in others you're a lot more like Mom's old station wagon. Many of your greatest challenges are in the "wagon" areas of your life. But those are the areas where I can really shine.

When the odds are stacked against you, let me take you to the finish line. When you feel that you might not be able to do it on your own, let me take the wheel and miraculously win through you. Then you can give me the glory.

Trust me in the wagon areas,
>God

== == ==   == == == == == == == == ==

GO FOR THE REAL THING

They exchanged the truth of God for a lie, and worshiped and served the creature rather than the Creator, who is blessed forever. Amen.

| Romans | 1:25 |

My Son,

>There is a difference between true Christianity and the cultural Christianity that comes with its own pale set of myths.

Jesus was a Jewish man from the Middle East, not a British actor portraying him in a film. The cross was a horrible way to die, not a pretty gold emblem on someone's necklace. When Jesus healed people, they didn't just receive a respectable prayer and a good feeling inside. They were radically prayed over and totally healed. When Jesus says that we have his power to accomplish things such as healing, he's not being figurative. "I'll be thinking about you, brother" doesn't cut it when someone's in need.

Son, don't settle for cultural Christianity when the real thing is available. My word is cross-cultural.

The Lord of the Undiluted Gospel,
>God

== == ==   == == == == == == == == ==

STAY PLUGGED IN

I am the vine, you are the branches; he who abides in Me and I in him, he bears much fruit.

John   15:5

My Son,

>My love and grace are meant to keep you fueled for your spiritual journey. But it's so easy to unplug from me, isn't it? It's easy to feel you've received enough power to go out on your own for a while. In a way that's true. Some people actually spend their whole spiritual lives using me like a battery charger rather than a constant power source. They power up at a retreat or an inspirational church service. Then they drift away and come back only when they're empty.

You can cruise on my power for a while without actually being connected to me. But that isn't the way I want you to live. The secret of the abundant, powerful life is staying connected to me. I designed you to live that way. So don't use me just for your spiritual recharge. Stay plugged in.

Your Source of Constant Power,
>God

== == ==   == == == == == == == == ==

THE CHICKEN OR THE EGG

Jesus Christ is the same yesterday and today and forever.

| Hebrews | 13:8 NIV |

My Son,

>Some people believe that I am just a figment of man's spiritual imagination. They believe that man created me in his mind in order to have a hope in something beyond himself. They seem confused as to whether I came first and created man to need me, or whether man came first and created me to meet his needs.

Well, let me put that question to rest. I came first, I came in the middle, and I will come again in the end. I existed before mankind could even feel or express a need. And in their darkest hour of need, I came into their world to meet their need through Jesus Christ. What's more, I will come again in the end to put all doubt to rest. At that point, everyone will be able to see and know the true order of creation. So worship me as the beginning, the middle, and the end.

The One Who Was and Is and Will Be,
>God

== == ==   == == == == == == == == ==

THE CURSE OF THE MOUNTAIN LION

**All these evil things proceed from
within and defile the man.**

Mark	7:23

My Son,

>Once a man built a beautiful home. While walking in the forest surrounding his house one day, he found a baby mountain lion abandoned by its mother. It was as cuddly as a domestic kitten, so he took it home, deciding to keep it until it got a little bigger. As the mountain lion grew, it sometimes would claw the man in play and hurt him. The man knew he should let the cat go, but by now he was very attached to it.

Soon the mountain lion became so large and aggressive it was destroying the house and hurting the man. By the time the man called the zoo to help him remove his "pet," it was totally out of control.

Son, habitual sin is like this. It starts as a cuddly curiosity, and by the time it becomes a full-blown problem, it is tearing your life apart. So don't reach for those curiosities. And if you've already invited something in, get help removing it.

The One Who Protects You,
>God

== == ==   == == == == == == == == ==

THE GIFT OF WILLINGNESS

Father, if You are willing, remove this cup from Me; yet not my will, but yours be done.

| Luke | 22:42 |

My Son,

>If Jesus had performed all of His miracles and wonders but begrudged laying down his life, he would have failed in his main earthly mission. His miracles and teaching blessed people in many ways. But it was that final act of obedience and surrender that accomplished my primary goal, the redemption of mankind.

There are lots of Christians who would love to be able to have the gift of healing or teaching or leading worship. Not nearly as many of them are willing to lay down their lives. A life totally yielded to me is what I'm looking for. When you're willing to lay it all down for me, when you're willing to pray daily, "Your will, not mine, O Lord," then you'll be the vessel ready for use in my kingdom.

Lord of the Willing Heart,
>God

== == ==   == == == == == == == == ==

THE SCRAP HEAP AND THE MASTERPIECE

Apart from Me you can do nothing.

| John | 15:5 NIV |

My Son,

>Do I confuse you when I say, "Apart from me, you can't do anything"?
You know you can do lots of things on your own. You drive a car,
work at a job, write a letter. So what do I mean?

The work you do on your own is like work done by a ten-year-old
holding a fine sculptor's chisel. Sure, the kid can hack a few primitive
forms out of wood. But place that same chisel in the hand of a master
sculptor, and art emerges. Once you see what the chisel can do when in
the master's hand, the childlike forms are thrown onto the scrap heap.

Son, I know you can do lots of things using the abilities I've given you.
But place yourself in my masterful hands, and what a difference! Don't
be satisfied with the scrap heap of human accomplishment. Commit
your life into my hands and discover the wonder of your true capabilities.

The Master Sculptor,
>God

== == ==   == == == == == == == == ==

YOUR GREATEST ACCOMPLISHMENT

If I speak in the tongues of men and of angels, but have not love, I am only a resounding gong or a clanging symbol.

1 Corinthians | 13:1 NIV

My Son,

>You can be a spiritual powerhouse, doing great miracles for me. You can constantly speak truth into other people's lives. You could give every extra cent you have to noble charities and even become a martyr for me. But if you aren't loving the people I've placed in your life, then you are just a big, loud advertisement for yourself.

Love is not a public display of spirituality. It is a private matter of the heart. The way you love the unlovely people is a mirror to your soul. Your opinion of others that only you and I know is the litmus test of true righteousness. Loving your family and meeting their emotional needs is the highest spiritual goal you should set.

Son, I have created you to accomplish wonderful things for me, but seek first to have a true heart of love for me and for others. That will be your greatest achievement of all.

The One Who Knows Your Heart,
>God

== == ==   == == == == == == == == ==

A MAN OF COMMITMENT

Therefore, I was not vacillating when I intended to do this, was I? Or what I purpose, do I purpose according to the flesh, so that with me there will be yes, yes and no, no at the same time?

2 Corinthians   1:17

My Son,

>So many people are afraid of commitment. There are too few in this modern age who will ever know the fulfillment of sticking with something for the long haul. People accept jobs and use them as strategic launching pads to other jobs, and their entire careers end up being leapfrog experiences.

Many who get tired of their mate move on to the next relationship. When their pastor hurts their feelings or says something they disagree with, they leave the church without even talking it out. Life has changed from a sit-down dinner into one big drive-through window.

In this age of fickle transience, I am calling on you to show the world what it is to make firm commitments and stick with them. Don't fall prey to the drive-through mentality. Sit down at the table of commitment and enjoy a long, satisfying meal.

The Lord of Commitment,
>God

== == ==   == == == == == == == == ==

AGE GRACEFULLY

I waste away; I will not live forever.
Leave me alone, for my days are but a breath.

Job	7:16

My Son,

>People in your culture are fascinated with keeping the human shell, the body, as youthful-looking as possible. But there is no fountain of physical youth. On earth, time is a tireless traveler. It marches on and inevitably catches up with you. This combination of time's inevitable passing and the culture's crazy obsession with youthfulness is a setup for depression when people reach or look a certain age.

But my kingdom is built not on an obsession with youthfulness but on a maturity principle. It esteems qualities that don't have anything to do with beauty or youth, qualities that show spiritual growth.

Son, don't try to cling to your youth. Embrace the aging process as part of life. I'm not concerned with how old you are but with how you age. I'm not concerned with your stage of life but with how well you're learning the lessons of each stage as you go through it.

The One Who Matures You,
>God

== == ==   == == == == == == == == ==

AN INCREDIBLE ENDING

Then the King will say to those on His right, "Come, you who are blessed of My Father, inherit the kingdom prepared for you from the foundation of the world. For I was hungry, and you gave Me something to eat; I was thirsty, and you gave Me something to drink; I was a stranger, and you invited Me in; naked, and you clothed Me; I was sick, and you visited Me; I was in prison, and you came to Me."

Matthew   25:34-36

My Son,

>There is an incredible ending to the Christian life on earth. Jesus is coming back for my faithful children. Then you will see him with your own eyes and worship him face to face. What an incredible time that will be! My children will know no more suffering or disease, no more wondering why things happened the way they did. Your aches and pains will be replaced with joy and peace. Though you have been lame, you will dance before me. Though you have suffered, you will be given laughter.

The most incredible thing about the ending of a Christian's life is that it is the beginning of an eternity of uninterrupted and total fulfillment. As you live your life on earth, no matter what your circumstances, you can have hope and courage, knowing that your life story will have a perfect ending. And that ending will be the beginning of eternity with me.

The Great King,
>God

== == ==   == == == == == == == == ==

AT AN ACCEPTABLE TIME

As for me, my prayer is to You, O Lord, at an acceptable time; O God, in the greatness of Your lovingkindness, answer me with Your saving truth.

| | Psalm | 69:13 | |

My Son,

>I am not your short-order cook. I don't always give you what you want when you think you should have it. I am more like the ultimate dietician who knows what you need and when you need it in order for your spiritual body to work at top performance. I know just the right combination of answered prayers that you need and when you need to receive them.

Prayer is not about placing an order and getting upset when it comes out all wrong or too late. It is about handing your spiritual diet over to the professional and trusting in the nourishment you receive. There is so much peace when you finally resign yourself and are able to pray, "O Lord, in your time, because you know what is best for me, answer me and give me what I need."

The One Who Knows Your Nutritional Needs,
>God

== == ==   == == == == == == == == ==

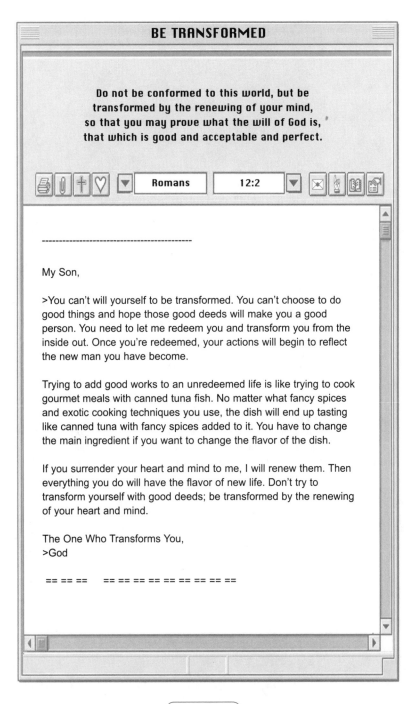

BE TRANSFORMED

Do not be conformed to this world, but be transformed by the renewing of your mind, so that you may prove what the will of God is, that which is good and acceptable and perfect.

Romans 12:2

My Son,

>You can't will yourself to be transformed. You can't choose to do good things and hope those good deeds will make you a good person. You need to let me redeem you and transform you from the inside out. Once you're redeemed, your actions will begin to reflect the new man you have become.

Trying to add good works to an unredeemed life is like trying to cook gourmet meals with canned tuna fish. No matter what fancy spices and exotic cooking techniques you use, the dish will end up tasting like canned tuna with fancy spices added to it. You have to change the main ingredient if you want to change the flavor of the dish.

If you surrender your heart and mind to me, I will renew them. Then everything you do will have the flavor of new life. Don't try to transform yourself with good deeds; be transformed by the renewing of your heart and mind.

The One Who Transforms You,
>God

== == == == == == == == == == ==

BEYOND YOUR BOUNDRIES

**With men it is impossible, but not with God:
for with God all things are possible.**

| Mark | 10:27 KJV |

My Son,

>I have great things planned for you, but it's going to involve your taking some chances. If you always play it safe, you will never experience the miracle of my work in you. If you are always swimming in pools where you're an arm's length from the edge, you won't experience the thrill of pushing past your limits.

I don't want you to live a reckless life, but I do want you to live a life that stretches you. Follow me beyond your own personal strengths and abilities to a place where the wonderful things that happen to you and through you can only be explained by my presence in your life. Don't limit yourself to what you can do easily and comfortably. Live life beyond your boundaries.

The Father of Limitless Possibilities,
>God

== == ==   == == == == == == == == ==

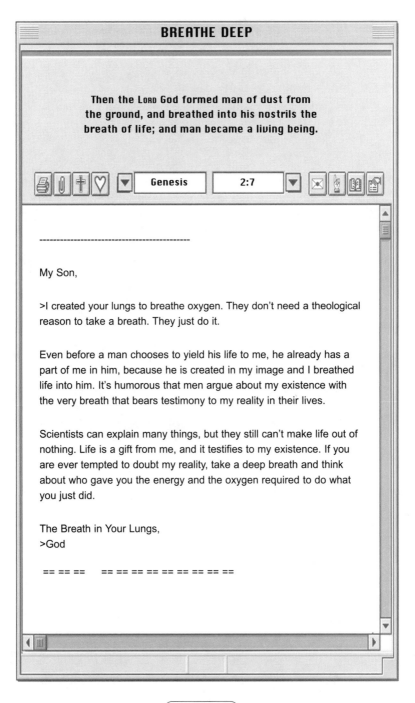

BREATHE DEEP

Then the Lord God formed man of dust from the ground, and breathed into his nostrils the breath of life; and man became a living being.

| Genesis | 2:7 |

My Son,

>I created your lungs to breathe oxygen. They don't need a theological reason to take a breath. They just do it.

Even before a man chooses to yield his life to me, he already has a part of me in him, because he is created in my image and I breathed life into him. It's humorous that men argue about my existence with the very breath that bears testimony to my reality in their lives.

Scientists can explain many things, but they still can't make life out of nothing. Life is a gift from me, and it testifies to my existence. If you are ever tempted to doubt my reality, take a deep breath and think about who gave you the energy and the oxygen required to do what you just did.

The Breath in Your Lungs,
>God

== == ==   == == == == == == == == ==

BUILD THE RUNWAY

So we built the wall and the whole wall was joined together to half its height, for the people had a mind to work.

Nehemiah   4:6

My Son,

>Many people want their dreams to carry them upward like an airplane. They sit around and refine these dreams, silently constructing and perfecting the "dreamcraft" they'll someday ride into the sky. But many times, these same people fail to spend any time constructing the solid runway that they'll need for that dream to take off.

An airplane can't take off without a runway, and dreams can't fly without practical plans and goals to launch them. I want you to be a dreamer, but I also want you to be a doer. Anyone can sit around and visualize himself in the cockpit, flying high. But without a down-to-earth plan, that dream will never take off. I have mile-high dreams for you, but I am calling you to do the day-to-day things that will make those dreams a reality. My call and your vision aren't enough. You need to dig in, live lean, and put it all on the table to build the runway. Then watch your dream take flight.

The One Who Gives You Dreams,
>God

== == ==   == == == == == == == == ==

CATERPILLARS AND GRACE

**I am confident of this very thing, that
He who began a good work in you will
perfect it until the day of Christ Jesus.**

| Philippians | 1:6 |

My Son,

>Everyone knows that caterpillars turn into butterflies eventually. But they are definitely caterpillars first. They can't fly; they move slowly; and they look like big, fat worms. But that's how they have to start out.

When you start your spiritual walk with me, I give you the promise of spiritual maturity, of healing, and of wholeness. But you aren't there yet. You are still a spiritual caterpillar. So stop beating yourself up for not being perfect and just keep moving toward the promise. I've created you to fly, but it is a process that takes time, patience, and lots of grace. In fact, no one ever truly comes into the fullness of that promise until he passes through the cocoon of death into my perfect kingdom. So live graciously in this caterpillar state, being the man I've created you to be and moving purposefully toward the promise of flight.

Your Creator,
>God

== == ==   == == == == == == == == ==

COME AND WORSHIP

Pray, then, in this way: "Our Father who is in heaven, hallowed be Your name."

| | Matthew | 6:9 | |

My Son,

>When you come to me, come with a worshipping heart. Come with thanksgiving on your lips and praise in your mouth. Don't do it because I need to be reminded of how good I am. I know how good I am. Having a worshipping heart reminds *you* of my goodness and helps set a framework for interaction with me. It tells you that I am God and you are not. It reminds you that every good thing you have has come down from me, your loving Father in Heaven. It reminds you of my holiness and your dependence on me.

Come and worship me because you were created to worship. You were created to respond to me with love and affection. You were created to say, "My father in Heaven, holy is your name." When you respond in this way, then you will know your place in the world and in my kingdom.

Come and worship,
>God

== == ==   == == == == == == == == ==

COME LIKE A CHILD

Whoever then humbles himself as this child, he is the greatest in the kingdom of heaven.

Matthew	18:4

My Son,

>I want you to come to me as a child comes to his loving father. I want to hold you like my son. I want to love you through the pain and wipe away the tears you cry in private. I want to cheer you on when you do something great. I want to laugh with you in the good times.

I am not a father who is hard to please. I'm always on your side. I am your biggest fan. I've been to every important event in your life, even when your earthly father wasn't there.

Sometimes when you're trying so hard to be a man, you may find it hard to come to me as a child. A child comes running to his father with reckless abandon. I will always open my arms to you, and I will always accept you. Run to me now.

Your Daddy,
>God

== == ==   == == == == == == == == ==

DON'T BE AFRAID TO ASK

**Where there is no guidance the people fall,
but in abundance of counselors there is victory.**

| | | | | | Proverbs | | 11:14 | | | | | |

My Son,

>My goal for you is that you have godly men around you to help you walk out your faith. No professional athlete ever became successful on his own. There was a line of coaches and trainers and teammates to help that athlete achieve his goals of winning. The Christian life is a race that you weren't meant to run alone. It takes godly coaching from mentors who can disciple you. It takes encouragement from teammates who are running the same race. It takes the healing touch of spiritual trainers who will take the time to pray for you and attend to your spiritual injuries.

I have created you to achieve the highest goal in Christ Jesus, but I didn't create you to do it alone. If you don't have mentors, teammates, and spiritual trainers in your life, let's seek them out together. Don't be afraid to ask for help in your spiritual walk. Help is what gets all winners to the finish line.

Your Biggest Fan,
>God

DON'T FEAR THE COOKIE CUTTER

Now, therefore, fear the Lord and serve Him in sincerity and truth; and put away the gods which your fathers served beyond the River and in Egypt, and serve the Lord.

Joshua 24:14

My Son,

>Many people stay away from me because they think that to become a Christian is to be cut out into the cookie-cutter shape of the Christian culture. They fear having to conform to unattractive Christian stereotypes. But there is no Christian cookie cutter. Christians are a group of very different people with a shared devotion and commitment to a person—Jesus Christ.

I don't expect you to align with a certain cause or political party or social school of thought. I don't expect you to change the way you dress or groom yourself. I only want you to be completely aligned with my Word, my Spirit, and my ministry on the earth.

Once you are aligned with me, I may give you a cause or a mission, but don't presuppose what it will be. I've created you as a unique being to have a unique faith, and I will show you how to carry that out. Don't fear the cookie cutter.

The One Who Created You Unique,
>God

== == ==   == == == == == == == == ==

DON'T HIDE THE BEDROOM

**The man and his wife were both
naked and were not ashamed.**

Genesis   2:25

My Son,

>I am the creator of romance and intimacy. I am the creator of love
and sexual relations. Why then do so many people think that I don't
know anything about sex?

It's because Satan won a battle in the Garden that he is still winning
today. He convinces men and women that they should be ashamed of
the intimate parts of their life and hide them from me because they
are shameful. As a result, many Christian couples worship me at
church but hide from me in the bedroom.

If you don't allow me to be Lord over everything, you're missing out. I
have a plan to make your intimate relationship with your wife the best that
it can be. Trust me with your love life, and the two of you will experience
greater intimacy than you ever have. Don't be ashamed to talk to me or
to your wife about it. Bring it all into the light, and be unashamed.

The Creator of Intimacy,
>God

== == ==   == == == == == == == == ==

DON'T SHY AWAY FROM CONFLICT

**"Present your case," the LORD says.
"Bring forward your strong arguments."**

Isaiah 41:21

My Son,

>Having conflict in your life is normal. Only dead people have no conflict in their lives. Some people tend to shy away from conflict because it makes them nervous. They believe if they ignore it, it will go away. But that just doesn't happen.

If you ignored a wound, it would become infected and lead to other problems. Ignoring it wouldn't make it go away. The same is true about difficult situations in your life.

I don't want you to shy away from conflict. It isn't bad if you handle it well. If you approach the situation with confidence in me and love toward the other person or people, then you have the power to heal or to prevent the wounds of conflict. Turn to me, and let's face conflict together.

Your Mediator,
>God

== == ==   == == == == == == == == ==

DREAMS MAY DIE, BUT THEN THE RESURRECTION

Truly, truly, I say to you, unless a grain of wheat falls into the earth and dies, it remains alone; but if it dies, it bears much fruit. He who loves his life loses it, and he who hates his life in this world will keep it to life eternal.

| | John | 12:24-25 | |

My Child,

>Sometimes you have to hand your dreams over to death in order to watch them be resurrected. A house that won't sell ends up keeping you in the same place to receive a blessing you couldn't have received otherwise. A promotion that goes to someone else ends up freeing you to make a better career move.

Trust your dreams to me, and I will never allow a door to close without opening another door. Jesus is the ultimate example. When he died on the cross and was laid in the tomb, the disciples had to let go of the kingdom he had promised. That door seemed closed. But when he rose to life again, a door of power and forgiveness was opened that would never have been possible had he not died. Son, yield yourself, as Jesus did, to my plans, and the doors you walk through will ultimately lead to blessing.

Trust me with your dreams,
>God

== == ==   == == == == == == == == ==

FAITH IS NOT THE SUSPENSION OF DOUBT

Until we all attain to the unity of the faith,
and of the knowledge of the Son of God, to
a mature man, to the measure of the stature
which belongs to the fullness of Christ.

Ephesians **4:13**

My Son,

>Whenever you drive your car or fly on an airplane, you are
exercising faith that you will arrive at your destination safely. Even if
you get scared during the trip or have doubts about your safe arrival,
your faith keeps you from losing all hope, pulling the emergency
hatch, and bailing out. Faith is not the suspension of doubt. It is rising
above doubt and going on faith until you arrive at the promise.

On the journey of life, as you experience some turbulence and
feelings of fear along the way, don't beat yourself up about doubting.
Just keep riding with the faith that keeps you on the journey. We will
arrive safely at our destination. Keep the faith.

The Lord of the Journey,
>God

== == ==   == == == == == == == == ==

FOLLOW THE PLAN

**Thus Noah did; according to all that
God had commanded him, so he did.**

Genesis   6:22

My Son,

>We are copartners in the building of your life. I am the architect and,
believe it or not, you are the main builder. I have the plan, and I am
leading you in the way you should build. But I can't build your life for
you. When you were in charge of your own life, you were trying to be
both architect and builder. But now that you've given me control, it's
time to get to work using my blueprints. I may tell you to tear down
things that you built to your own specifications, or I may tell you to
rewire your whole life; but you have to trust me.

Once we demolish the things that were out of order, it's time to move
on toward my perfect plan for erecting what is beautiful and lasting
and strong. I will help you and guide you a brick at a time, but it takes
your hard work as well as my plan. Let's build this thing right.

The Architect of a Wonderful Life,
>God

== == ==   == == == == == == == == ==

FORGIVE YOUR DEBTORS

Forgive us our debts, as we also have forgiven our debtors.

Matthew 6:12 NIV

My Son,

>If you are grateful for the way I forgive your sins, please be forgiving to those who sin against you. It is easy to understand this concept, but it's so hard to live it out. Why? Because once someone sins against you, he places power in your hands to either forgive him or to withhold that forgiveness. And whenever a human being is placed in the power position, it is always tempting to wield that power rather than lay it down and forgive.

I want you to forgive as I forgave you. I had the ultimate power to withhold forgiveness from mankind for sinning against me, but I laid down that power at the cross and said, "I will forgive." If you are tempted to hold on to unforgiveness, take it to the cross. Lay it down and forgive.

The One Who Forgave You,
>God

== == ==   == == == == == == == == ==

FREE INDEED

So if the Son makes you free,
you will be free indeed.

| John | 8:36 |

My Son,

>A prisoner who breaks out of jail isn't truly free. He lives the rest of his life using a false identity, looking over his shoulder, trying to stay one step ahead of the law. But a prisoner who is pardoned by a government leader can walk out of jail and taste complete freedom.

Many men think that they can break free from the consequences of sin on their own. They say, "I'm a free man. What do I need with God's forgiveness?" But this sort of self-salvation becomes an internal running game from the truth and the law. Instead of acknowledging his true identity as a sinner in need of a savior, such a man assumes a false identity as a free man and spends his life running from me.

True freedom can be found only in being pardoned from your sin by Jesus Christ. Then you can walk out of the prison of your sin and never look back. Ask for my pardon and be set free.

The One Who Pardons You,
>God

== == ==   == == == == == == == == ==

LET IT COME FORTH

The fruit of the Spirit is love, joy, peace, patience, kindness, goodness, faithfulness, gentleness, self-control; against such things there is no law.

Galatians 5:22–23

My Son,

>A fruit tree doesn't will itself to produce fruit. It doesn't make up its mind and struggle until fruit finally appears on its branches. No, fruit comes forth and ripens as a tree puts down roots toward the water and lifts its branches toward the sun.

In the same way, spiritual fruit in your life doesn't appear as a result of your struggling or your self-will. You don't say to yourself one day, "OK, I'm really going to have joy now," and then struggle until you're joyful. But if you focus on me, putting down roots into the living water of my truth and lifting your life to my Son, then you will begin to see the fruit of the Spirit spring to life naturally in you.

So don't try to produce spiritual fruit on your own. Relax, drink deeply of my goodness, worship me, and see the fruit come forth.

The Producer of Fruit,
>God

== == ==   == == == == == == == == ==

GET OUT OF "SINSVILLE"

Lot went out and spoke to his sons-in-law, who
were to marry his daughters, and said, "Up, get
out of this place, for the LORD will destroy the city."
But he appeared to his sons-in-law to be jesting.

| Genesis | 19:14 |

My Son,

>The movies have created a stereotype of a Christian doomsayer foaming at the mouth and wearing an apocalyptic message on a poster around his neck. This type of character is meant to be comical in the movies. But don't let that keep you from hearing me when I give you a real-life convicting word, saying, "Get out of this place; it's going to be the death of you."

I don't joke about things that matter. Sin is real and its effects on you are equally real. I will never allow you to die in your sin. I will always give you a warning message and provide a way out of "Sinsville." But if you don't take that warning seriously and repent and move on quickly, you may suffer real (even deadly) consequences.

Sin is no laughing matter. When you hear my warning, repent and get out of Sinsville.

The One Who Provides a Way Out,
>God

GODLY AMBITION

They said, "Come, let us build for ourselves a city, and a tower whose top will reach into heaven, and let us make for ourselves a name, otherwise we will be scattered abroad over the face of the whole earth."

Genesis 11:4

My Son,

>I have given you a drive and a godly ambition to achieve my purposes for your life. I have given you the raw materials and provided you with the skills to build a mighty kingdom for me on the earth. But if you take those skills and choose to build a tower that lifts yourself up so that everyone can see you, then you are off track.

There is nothing wrong with gaining the respect of other people. But putting your own name in lights should never be your goal. Instead, what you build should point to my presence in your life. Try to make every project and every accomplishment another opportunity to give me glory. Then you will have achieved the true goal of your God-given ambition.

Keep pointing to me,
>God

== == ==   == == == == == == == == ==

GRAB THE LIFELINE

He brought me up out of the pit of destruction,
out of the miry clay, and He set my feet
upon a rock making my footsteps firm.

| | | | Psalm | | 40:2 | | | | |

My Son,

>When Christians say that they have been saved, they aren't
exaggerating. Sin is kind of like the canoe trip from hell. It starts off
being peaceful and inviting. Then the pace picks up. After a while,
you're trapped in the rapids, blind to the huge drop-off that threatens
to crush you on the jagged rocks below. Salvation can be a conviction
I give when you're in the still waters, telling you that you're heading
for trouble. Or it can be the helicopter that scoops you up right before
you tumble into oblivion.

When people say that they were "saved," that's exactly what
happened. A person caught in the rapids of sin is bound to end up
over the edge without intervention. I sent Jesus as a lifeline to those
who are heading for destruction. Because of him, you don't have to
be swept over the edge. You can be lifted out and set on solid
ground. If you feel as if you're being swept away, grab the lifeline.

The One Who Saves You,
>God

== == ==   == == == == == == == == ==

HUNTING DOWN THE TRUTH

Roam to and fro through the streets of Jerusalem, and look now and take note. And seek in her open squares, if you can find a man, if there is one who does justice, who seeks truth, then I will pardon her.

| Jeremiah | 5:1 |

My Son,

>It takes a skilled hunter to find the truth, because many times truth can be a wild, evasive animal. I don't want you to be like the spiritually lazy, who are content to sit back at the hunting lodge and have someone else's belief prepared and fed to them. I want you to be one of those rugged individuals who has the burning desire to stare reality in the face and wrestle it to the ground.

I have given you the mental ability and the supernatural insight to know the truth about spiritual things. With my Word and Spirit as your guides, you will be able to chase that truth down, subdue it, consume it, and share it with others. There will always be some answers that get away, but don't give up the hunt.

Your Father,
>God

== == ==   == == == == == == == == ==

I DON'T ALWAYS CALM THE STORM

The waves of death encompassed me; the torrents of destruction overwhelmed me; the cords of Sheol surrounded me; the snares of death confronted me. In my distress I called upon the LORD, yes, I cried to my God; and from His temple He heard my voice, and my cry for help came into His ears.

| 2 Samuel | 22:5-7 |

My Son,

>I don't always calm the storms of your life, but I do always give you an opportunity to have peace in the midst of those storms. Having peace inside doesn't have to depend on what's going on outside. Peace is the gift of knowing that you are mine and that I will guide you through each storm safely. If your job seems like a tidal wave of stress coming to swamp your peace, it can get you only as wet as you let it. If financial strain threatens to run you aground, you have the option to let me expand your shallows with my deep provision.

You have a choice to steady yourself in me. Once you become assured that I won't let you down, then each storm becomes a strengthening experience and each challenge becomes a faith builder. Don't always look for the storm to die down. Stabilize yourself through prayer, scripture, worship, and fellowship. Then you will have my peace that can weather any storm.

Your Peace,
>God

== == ==   == == == == == == == == ==

I STAND AT THE DOOR

Behold, I stand at the door and knock; if anyone
hears My voice and opens the door, I will come
in to him and will dine with him, and he with Me.

Revelation 3:20

My Son,

>I stand at the door of your heart and knock. But whether you open
the door or not depends on how you interpret the knock. If you view
me as a lawman waiting to make you pay for your crimes, then you'll
bolt your door fast and hide inside. If you see me as the spiritual
bounty hunter, coming to kick the door of your heart down and drag
you off to jail, you'll never trust me.

But if you see me as I am, you will fling the door open wide. I am a
friend who brings an incredible meal that we can share. It is the meal
of forgiveness and the wine of pardon. I am a gentleman who will
respect your choice, but I won't go away, because I know the
goodness of what I bring. Open the door of your heart to me.

I wait at the door,
>God

== == ==   == == == == == == == == ==

I WILL GIVE YOU WHAT YOU NEED

What man is there among you who, when his son asks for a loaf, will give him a stone? Or if he asks for a fish, he will not give him a snake, will he?

Matthew 7:9-10

My Son,

>I am not your prayer genie. I am not here to fulfill every one of your wishes. My promise to you was that through Christ Jesus, I will provide all of your needs, not all of your wants.

Because I desire the best for you, I won't always give you whatever you ask for. A good father would never give his child something harmful. In the same way, I will never grant a request that I know will bring you harm.

I want you to pray in accordance with my Spirit and my will, not your own desires. Don't just pray that I would help your softball team win; pray that everyone on the opposing side would come to know me. Don't pray for a new luxury car; pray that you would be able to drive in traffic without getting angry. Pray about things that matter, and I will respond with things that are in your best interest.

The One Who Answers Your Prayers,
>God

== == ==   == == == == == == == == ==

LET THE WATER FLOW

He said, "Thus says the Lord, 'Make this valley full of trenches.'
For thus says the Lord, 'You shall not see wind nor shall you
see rain; yet that valley shall be filled with water, so that
you shall drink, both you and your cattle and your beasts.'"

2 Kings   3:16–17

My Son,

>I have a huge reserve of miraculous, overcoming, healing water that
I want to pour out in your life. But you are the pipe and faucet that my
holy water has to flow through, and you choose the speed and the
amount of that flow. You can choose to shut me off in your life. But if
you do, you won't get the benefits of feeling my purifying stream
cleaning you on the inside and then flowing through you into the lives
of those around you.

I encourage you to open yourself up fully to my holy presence flowing
in and through you. Don't tighten the valves of your heart and shut off
the flow. Be my pipeline of healing and salvation to the world.

Waiting to Send the Waters,
>God

== == ==   == == == == == == == == ==

I'M BRINGING MY KINGDOM

**Your kingdom come. Your will be done,
on earth as it is in heaven.**

| | Matthew | 6:10 | |

My Son,

>Some people come to me and ask, "What are you doing, God? I thought you would do things differently." What they really mean is, "I could run things a lot better than you, God." These prayers accomplish less than nothing.

Here is the prayer that pleases me: "O God, how can I get in line with what you're doing? How can I line up with your will?" I want you to know the freedom of trusting my plans instead of pulling against them.

My tactics for bringing my kingdom to the earth may not always make sense to you. But you will have to choose how you will respond to them. You can either stand around and question my plans, or you can work with me to accomplish them. Choose to know the incredible joy of resigning yourself to my will by saying, "Your kingdom come, your will be done."

The Kingdom-bringer,
>God

== == ==   == == == == == == == == ==

YOU ARE MY BUSINESS

He counts the number of the stars; He calls them
all by name. Great is our Lord, and mighty
in power; His understanding is infinite.

| | Psalm | 147:4-5 | |

My Son,

>I am not a busy father, rushing off to my office in the sky where I
have bigger things to think about than you. Often people think, *God
has the whole universe to worry about. I'm not going to bother him
with something I can probably figure out on my own.* But that's not the
way I want you to think. I want to be involved in every aspect of your
life. I long to give you guidance on every decision and insight into
every problem. Through me, you have access to infinite wisdom. Let's
sit down and have a board meeting about your life.

You are my business. You don't ever have to go through a problem
alone again. Turn to me and ask for guidance. You have my ear and
my attention.

Working with You,
>God

== == ==   == == == == == == == == ==

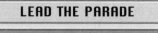
LEAD THE PARADE

Then it happened as the ark of the LORD came into the city of David that Michal the daughter of Saul looked out of the window and saw King David leaping and dancing before the LORD; and she despised him in her heart.

| | 2 Samuel | 6:16 | |

My Son,

>David was the most esteemed man in all of Israel. He was a hero in battle and a hero in my heart. He was the king of Israel bringing the ark of the covenant into Israel, a crowning achievement in his political career. But he didn't just appoint the Billy Graham of his day to give the prayer for the occasion while he sat stiffly by in a suit watching the procession. Instead, he dressed up in the equivalent of running shorts and led the parade, dancing and singing praises to me. Can you imagine the leader of your nation doing that today?

Son, I don't lift men up and make them honorable just so they can sit around acting stuffy. I lift men up so they can freely give me glory and point others to me. Don't fall into the trap of trying to act respectable. When my parade comes to town, I want you at the front, dancing with all of your might.

The One Worthy of All of Your Worship,
>God

== == ==   == == == == == == == == ==

LET'S SPEND SOME TIME TOGETHER

The Lord answered and said to her, "Martha, Martha, you are worried and bothered about so many things; but only one thing is necessary, for Mary has chosen the good part, which shall not be taken away from her."

Luke 10:41-42

My Son,

>If you really loved someone and hadn't seen them in a while, would you want them to rush around cleaning and cooking and fussing over you, or would you want them to sit down, have a cup of coffee with you, and just talk for a while?

Busy Christians are often perceived to be the most spiritual Christians. Many times they are also the most successful in the eyes of the church and the world, so they are lifted up and imitated. This is unfortunate, because doing things for me will never substitute for just hanging out with me.

I want to spend quality time with you. If you seek to do things in my name, make sure they are done out of a deep identity of friendship with and acceptance from me. There's no need to fuss around looking spiritual in order to gain my acceptance. You've already got my acceptance. Now let's sit down and spend some time together.

Your Friend,
>God

== == ==   == == == == == == == == ==

ENJOY THE LIFE I'VE GIVEN YOU

God saw all that he had made, and it was very good.

| Genesis | 1:31 NIV |

My Son,

>Life is something I created for you to take joy in. It's not a necessary medicine that you have to struggle to get down while waiting for your heavenly homecoming. It should be like a cool drink of lemonade on a hot afternoon, refreshing and delicious.

I want you to open your eyes to the wonderful things I've created for you to experience. Take delight in the beauty of a sunset. Lie down on a freshly cut lawn and smell the grass. Enjoy the people I've placed in your life. Celebrate their uniqueness. Share your joy with them. When you begin to see life as an amazing gift, you will be able to enter fully into the beauty and joy of my creation.

The Wonder of Life,
>God

== == ==   == == == == == == == == ==

LIGHT AS A FEATHER

As far as the east is from the west, so far has He removed our transgressions from us.

Psalm 103:12 NIV

My Son,

>Sometimes you fail. Sometimes you let people down. Sometimes you even let me down. But I will always forgive you, even if people won't. If you are feeling guilty about something, maybe something you've been carrying around for a while, there's no need to hold on to that guilt for one more minute.

The guilt that you hold on to seems as if it weighs a million pounds. But once you place it in my hands and ask for forgiveness, that guilt becomes as light as a feather and I blow it away, as far as the east is from the west. Come to me now, confess your sin and guilt, and place them in my hands. Then watch that feather fly away.

Your Forgiving Father,
>God

== == ==   == == == == == == == == ==

PRAYER IS A TWO-WAY CONVERSATION

**My sheep hear my voice, and I
know them, and they follow me.**

John   10:27 KJV

My Son,

>Many people think that prayer is talking to me about things on your
heart. But that's only half of what happens in prayer. Prayer is a
conversation between two people. I want to hear what's going on in
your life, and I want to hear your requests. But I've also got lots of
things I want to say to you. I want to talk to you. I want to tell you how
much I love you, to give you daily direction, to laugh with you, and to
share my heart with you.

Set aside some time each day for me to speak to you. Be patient;
tune your ear in to my voice, and wait for me to speak. Don't be
frustrated if you don't hear me right away. I am not like the television
set, on which everything moves quickly and everyone speaks loudly. I
speak in a still, gentle voice to your heart. Let's begin a daily
conversation of prayer.

Are you listening?
>God

== == ==   == == == == == == == == ==

RESPECT THOSE WHO CAME BEFORE

You shall rise up before the grayheaded and honor the aged, and you shall revere your God; I am the Lord.

Leviticus 19:32

My Son,

>People in modern society do not tend to honor their elders. Youth and beauty rule the television, and older people are often depicted as jokes or irrelevant props to the main story.

Son, I am calling all of my children to honor their elders. Don't buy into the story line that people over sixty-five are washed up. In fact, the exact opposite is true. Their wisdom and spiritual insight are invaluable to society and to the church. I set it up so that those who came before should lead those who come after, and that the youth should seek the counsel of their elders. Be a man who respects your elders and reaps the benefits of their wisdom and counsel. When you honor your elders, you honor me.

The Great Elder,
>God

== == ==   == == == == == == == == ==

SAVE THE BEST FOR HOME

Enjoy life with the woman whom you love all the days of your fleeting life which He has given to you under the sun; for this is your reward in life and in your toil in which you have labored under the sun.

Ecclesiastes 9:9

My Son,

>As many men get older, they trade their spontaneity and creativity for duty and responsibility. I don't want you to fall into that trap.

If your wife's need for love and acceptance is second place to your boss's need for productivity, then your priorities are out of balance. If your desire to knock a couple of points off of your golf game is greater than your desire to invest time in boosting your kids' self-esteem, something is backwards. When your work, your buddies, and your hobbies get the best parts of you, then what your family gets are the leftovers.

I have made you a wonderful person, and I want your family to get the greatest benefit from you. I also want you to get the greatest benefit from them. This can happen only if you place your relationship with them above your golf score. If you feel you are giving most of yourself away to other things, make a new commitment to save the best for home.

Your Father,
>God

== == ==   == == == == == == == == ==

STAND FIRM AND FIGHT

Stand firm therefore, having girded your loins with truth, and having put on the breastplate of righteousness, and having shod your feet with the preparation of the gospel of peace; in addition to all, taking up the shield of faith with which you will be able to extinguish all the flaming arrows of the evil one.

Ephesians   6:14–16

My Son,

>The armor I have given to equip you for spiritual battle is made up almost entirely of offensive weapons. I didn't give you the "backplate" of retreat to guard you as you run away from the battle. I didn't give you the foxhole of spiritual hiding. I have equipped you to be proactive in your faith, not reactive. I want you to hold the truth close and live the truth in righteousness. I want you to stand ready to share the truth with others and always hold the protective shield of faith that you may believe fully in me, the one who leads you into battle.

If you feel like slacking off in your faith and taking a little retreat, don't do it. The spiritual armor I have given you makes it safer to face the challenges of life than to run away from them. If you will just hold firm and fight, you will have all the protection you need.

The One Who Forges Your Armor,
>God

== == ==   == == == == == == == == ==

STEP OFF THE STAGE

When you give to the poor, do not let your left hand know what your right hand is doing, so that your giving will be in secret; and your Father who sees what is done in secret will reward you.

| Matthew | 6:3-4 |

My Son,

>It's tempting at times to join the ranks of the Christian "superstars." A Christian superstar makes it very obvious when he is doing and serving and giving and blessing. But the term Christian superstar is really an oxymoron.

In my kingdom, the least will be the greatest. Pride and humility can't live side by side in a Christian. So when you do a good deed, do it because I am watching and taking joy in it. Don't do it for your own glory in the eyes of other people. Step off the superstar stage and become a behind-the-scenes performer for an audience of one—me.

The One Who Knows Your Heart,
>God

== == ==   == == == == == == == == ==

THE BLESSING OF CONTENTMENT

Godliness actually is a means of great gain when accompanied by contentment. For we have brought nothing into the world, so we cannot take anything out of it either. If we have food and covering, with these we shall be content.

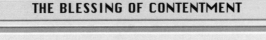

| 1 Timothy | | 6:6-8 |

My Son,

>I am not a spiritual slot machine from which, if you get your life aligned just right, blessings will pour like silver dollars. I don't want you to come to me because you want a financial blessing in your life. I want you to come to me because you want to have a relationship with me. The riches of my kingdom that come down to my godly children aren't necessarily financial. They are the riches of contentment.

When you are in right relationship with me, you will be content no matter what your circumstances. I don't want you to sit around and pray, looking forward to the day when I will truly bless you. I want you to praise me for the provision I have already given you. This is true even if I only meet your basic needs for the rest of your life. Stop seeking to cash in on your relationship with me. A man of contentment is the richest man of all.

Seek me for me,
>God

== == ==　== == == == == == == == ==

THE CALL OF THE DEEP

**Deep calls unto deep at the noise
of Your waterfalls.**

Psalm   42:7 NKJV

My Son,

>If you were a deep-sea sailor, you wouldn't be satisfied floating in a raft in the shallow end of a backyard pool. This manufactured, miniature scenario wouldn't satisfy your call to be out on the deep ocean.

In the same way, I have created your heart to sail the deep spiritual seas. The depth of my Spirit calls to the deep part of your heart. If you spend your life floating in the backyard pool of shallow, worldly thinking, commercialism, and carnal pleasures, you will never have the satisfaction you long for. To find true fulfillment, you must answer the call of the deep.

Deeper Than the Oceans,
>God

== == ==   == == == == == == == == ==

THE DEPTHS OF PEACE

He must ask in faith without any doubting, for the one who doubts is like the surf of the sea, driven and tossed by the wind.

James 1:6

My Son,

>When a storm is tossing the ocean, it is really only affecting the very top part of that water. The creatures living in the deep are so protected that they can't even tell that there is a storm. Because you know me, you have the inroad to peace. Even when the storms rage on the surface of your life, the depths of my love are always peaceful and serene.

But your peace depends on where you chose to live. If you are used to having your peace be circumstantial, then you will always be blown about by the changing tides on the surface of life. But if you are trusting me and living in my deep peace, the wind can blow and the rains can fall, but nothing will touch the depths of your peace. Choose today to go deep and live in my peace.

I'll meet you in the depths,
>God

== == ==   == == == == == == == == ==

THE FIRE OF REAL LOVE

This is the will of God, your sanctification; that is, that you abstain from sexual immorality; that each of you know how to possess his own vessel in sanctification and honor, not in lustful passion, like the Gentiles who do not know God.

1 Thessalonians — 4:3-5

My Son,

>Don't be fooled by the disguise of lust. Lust is like lighter fluid on a piece of paper. It burns fast and furiously without producing any lasting heat. When it's burning, it seems like the real thing, but once it dies, it is so obvious that it wasn't.

But real love is more like a hickory wood fire. It takes time, patience, and hard work to build it, but once it is roaring, its deep embers will burn, constant and hot, for a lifetime if you continue to maintain it.

This is the love that I want you to experience in your life with your spouse. Don't fall, like so many men, into the trap of the quick, easy fire of premarital and extramarital lust. Take the time to build and maintain real love in your life, and you will never be left out in the cold. (Boys play with matches, but men build fires.)

The Creator of Long-burning Love,
>God

== == ==   == == == == == == == == ==

THE FREEDOM OF GUIDELINES

**Those whom I love, I reprove and chasten;
so be zealous and repent.**

Revelation | 3:19 RSV

My Child,

>The United States is based on ideas of freedom and liberty. U.S. citizens tend to get nervous about any law that threatens to restrict their personal freedom. But freedom is not the absence of rules and laws. In fact, freedom is made possible by them. If America had no constitution and no governing body, it would have been conquered long ago. If money had no set value, you couldn't use it to buy anything. If there were no law enforcement, you wouldn't feel free to go outside your house without the fear of being mugged. There is comfort in knowing the law of the land and trusting in its rules.

I have set up a spiritual nation much greater than the United States. It is based on guidelines I set up to increase your safety and liberty, not to restrict your personal freedom. Because you know that I'm a just God and a loving Father, you can take comfort in the law of my kingdom.

Your Freedom,
>God

== == ==   == == == == == == == == ==

THE FULLNESS OF GOD

So that Christ may dwell in your hearts through faith; and that you, being rooted and grounded in love, may be able to comprehend with all the saints what is the breadth and length and height and depth, and to know the love of Christ which surpasses knowledge, that you may be filled up to all the fullness of God.

Ephesians **3:17-19**

My Son,

>Do you want to know how to be filled with all of my fullness? It's not something you can study in school. It's not something you have to search for in a far-off land. It is something that occurs inside of you when you have a supernatural awakening to the reality of how much I really love you.

This takes a miracle of understanding because my love is broader, longer, higher, and deeper than humans can understand. I send a superhuman love to fill human containers. It is not a conditional love; it is not a meet-you-halfway love. It is an all-consuming, all-accepting, every-corner-of-your-soul kind of love. Bible studies will educate you, and worship services will inspire you; but only my love opens the door to my fullness.

Pray for a full understanding of my love. Once you open your heart to receive more than it can hold and open your mind to reach beyond its capabilities, you'll be on your way to being filled with my fullness.

Know how much I love you,
>God

WITH YOU IN THE DESERT

"Behold, I will stand before you there on the rock
at Horeb; and you shall strike the rock, and water
will come out of it, that the people may drink."
And Moses did so in the sight of the elders of Israel.

Exodus 17:6

My Son,

>For a long time, the promised land was just that: a promise. The Israelites lived many years as captives in Egypt, only to be led into a sweltering desert for many more years. In the same way, I led you out of your spiritual captivity, but sometimes you find yourself in a spiritual desert.

Well, sometimes the way to the promised land is through the desert. Even though I don't always lead you to the place of easy blessing, I can miraculously sustain you in the desert times.

If you find yourself in a spiritual desert today, don't complain about not being dropped right into the promised land. Instead, cry out to me and let me pour out my waters of refreshing even in the driest places of your life. I am with you in the desert.

The Waters of Refreshing,
>God

== == ==   == == == == == == == == ==

THE REPRESENTATION OR THE REAL THING

I am with you always, even to the end of the age.

Matthew | 28:20 NKJV

My Son,

>If you had to be away from home for a while, and you had a choice, would you take pictures and home videos of your loved ones so you would remember their faces, or would you take *them* with you?

To many men, I am represented in a million works of art, stained-glass windows, crucifixes, statues, and other memorabilia. I am a historical memory they left behind, and a far-away promise they can hardly remember. But to those who know me, I am with them wherever they go.

I am not just a picture to look at until we are together again. I am with you right now. Don't settle for the memorabilia. Choose the relationship.

Take me with you,
>God

== == ==   == == == == == == == == ==

THE SPIRITUAL BATTLE

Our struggle is not against flesh and blood, but against the rulers, against the powers, against the world forces of this darkness, against the spiritual forces of wickedness in the heavenly places.

Ephesians   **6:12**

My Son,

>You are fighting a spiritual battle against the forces of Satan, even though you can't see it with your eyes. And that battle is being waged for the souls of men and women. Since I have chosen you to be a strong warrior for my causes, I want to tell you a secret to spiritual strength in battle.

The weapons you use are weapons of love, not traditional weapons of war. The strongest man on the battlefield is the one who has admitted his total weakness and dependence on me. The power position is on your knees in prayer. Humility is strength, and perseverance is power.

Satan will work subtly to tell you that only a mighty man who is strong in his own strength can win this battle. He knows that when you are puffed up with pride and self-importance, you are the easiest target of all. Stay weak in yourself but strong in me. Stay humble and trusting and ready for the long haul.

Your General,
>God

== == ==   == == == == == == == == ==

THE WELLSPRING OF LIFE

**Above all else, guard your heart,
for it is the wellspring of life.**

| Proverbs | 4:23 NIV |

My Son,

>If you had a flowing spring on your land so fresh you could drink from it, you would guard the purity of that spring because it would give life to everything around it. You wouldn't allow anything dead or decaying to be near the source because it would affect the purity of its outflow.

Your heart is the wellspring of life in you. You should guard its purity because what flows out from it affects the rest of your life. If you look at pornography or violence or turn yourself over to greed or jealousy, you are throwing dead, decaying animals in the water. They will slowly poison the purity of your heart and begin to destroy everything around you. Fantasy and internal compromise might seem harmless, but when they flow out, they have an effect on your world. So guard the spring of your heart, and it will flow purely and bring life to everything and everyone around.

The Living Water,
>God

== == ==   == == == == == == == == ==

TUNE IN

Eli said to Samuel, "Go lie down, and it shall be if He calls you, that you shall say, 'Speak, LORD, for Your servant is listening.'" So Samuel went and lay down in his place.

| | 1 Samuel | 3:9 | |

My Son,

>There is a God frequency that your heart can tune in to. I am sending out messages twenty-four hours a day, seven days a week to mankind. In the old days, I spoke to my people through a few prophets who had their dial set correctly to my voice. Because they could hear me, they spoke for me to the Israelites. But now that Jesus has come to you, every man who believes in him has the ability to tune in to me like a prophet and hear my voice.

You are my incredible son. I want you to be able to hear me when I speak to you. Begin to tune in through prayer and quiet meditation. Once you have established the connection, you will have the words of life and the music of Heaven. Tune in.

The Constant Message,
>God

== == ==   == == == == == == == == ==

TURN ON THE LIGHTS

Your word is a lamp to my feet and a light to my path.

Psalm 119:105

My Son,

>Would you ever drive your car at night without turning your headlights on first? Of course you wouldn't. If you did, you would be setting yourself up for an accident.

Life can become confusing and dark sometimes, and it is impossible to navigate without some source of light to show the way. The Bible is a navigation lamp for traveling through the dark challenges of life. Just as you don't debate about whether to turn your headlights on when it's dark, I want you to come to my Word, instinctively knowing that it will light your way. Spend some time each day opening up the Bible, asking me for direction, and reading what I have to say. Miraculously, you will begin to see life more clearly than you ever have before.

Before you go out into the darkness of the world, turn on the light of my Word.

The One Who Lights Your Path,
>God

== == ==   == == == == == == == == ==

UNWRAP THE TRUE GIFT

By grace you have been saved through faith; and that not of yourselves, it is the gift of God.

Ephesians | 2:8

My Son,

>Maybe you can remember some Christmas mornings in your childhood when all the presents and the wrapping paper still left you feeling vaguely unsatisfied. That remaining emptiness was telling you that there was more to life than just your wish list.

I gave you the gift of Jesus on his birthday. The gift was wrapped in dirty cloths, not fancy paper. He came fully assembled and didn't need batteries for power. He is the only gift that brings true and lasting satisfaction. Once you have unwrapped him in your heart, you're done. There's no more looking around for something better. Receive my gift. Your wish list will be mysteriously fulfilled and your needs truly met.

The Gift and the Giver,
>God

== == ==   == == == == == == == == ==

WHAT'S IN YOUR WOODPILE?

Finally, brethren, whatever is true, whatever is honorable, whatever is right, whatever is pure, whatever is lovely, whatever is of good repute, if there is any excellence and if anything worthy of praise, dwell on these things.

| Philippians | 4:8 |

My Son,

>What you take into your mind and spirit matters. You are building a spiritual house with the raw materials that you place in your woodpile. If you keep piling up rotten, termite-infested lumber, then the house you are building will fall apart. If you are placing anger, impatience, impurity, and slander in your spiritual woodpile, then the result will be a structural disaster. But if you are stockpiling peace, love, and holiness, the lumber you grab for will always be strong and sure.

Son, I want you to build a sturdy fortress of faith. If you are wondering why your spiritual house is in poor condition, look at the woodpile from which you've been getting your supplies. Call on me, the great Carpenter. Together we can throw out the bad materials and begin to reconstruct, using the things that will build a solid house of beauty and protection.

The Great Carpenter,
>God

== == ==   == == == == == == == == ==

YOU ARE UNIQUE

My frame was not hidden from Thee, when I was made in secret, and skillfully wrought in the depths of the earth.

| | Psalm | 139:15 | |

My Son,

>After I made you, I broke the mold. I burned the blueprints. There is not another person on the face of the earth that is exactly like you. You are a unique creation, beautiful in my sight.

Rejoice in your uniqueness. Don't try to imitate other people, and don't feel embarrassed about anything that I have created in you. Instead, begin to embrace who you are and begin to live in my distinctive plan for your life. Once you begin to walk in that plan, you will understand certain things about yourself that you never understood before. Your shortcomings will become blessings, and your gifts will become tools in my hand. Delight in all that I've created you to be, my perfect creation.

Your Creator,
>God

== == ==   == == == == == == == == ==

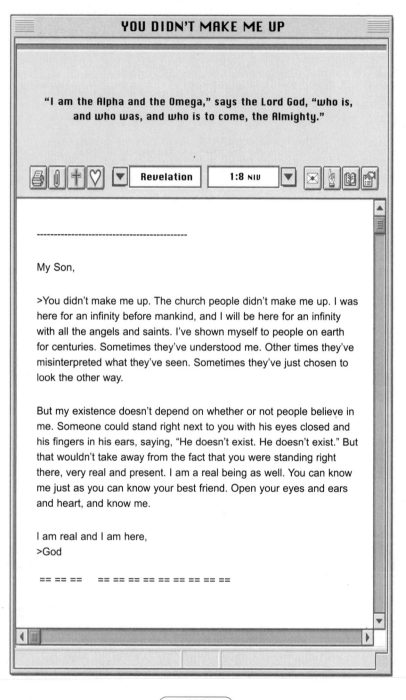

YOU DIDN'T MAKE ME UP

"I am the Alpha and the Omega," says the Lord God, "who is, and who was, and who is to come, the Almighty."

Revelation 1:8 NIV

My Son,

>You didn't make me up. The church people didn't make me up. I was here for an infinity before mankind, and I will be here for an infinity with all the angels and saints. I've shown myself to people on earth for centuries. Sometimes they've understood me. Other times they've misinterpreted what they've seen. Sometimes they've just chosen to look the other way.

But my existence doesn't depend on whether or not people believe in me. Someone could stand right next to you with his eyes closed and his fingers in his ears, saying, "He doesn't exist. He doesn't exist." But that wouldn't take away from the fact that you were standing right there, very real and present. I am a real being as well. You can know me just as you can know your best friend. Open your eyes and ears and heart, and know me.

I am real and I am here,
>God

== == ==   == == == == == == == == ==

FEELING AND DOING

This is what the Sovereign Lord, the Holy One of Israel,
says: "In repentance and rest is your salvation,
in quietness and trust is your strength."

Isaiah 30:15 NIV

Dear Child,

>Some people have the mistaken idea that to repent is to feel bad about their sins. But to repent is *not* to *feel* something; it's to *do* something. To repent is to turn around, to change your course and go at life from a different direction.

Suppose you discovered that you had taken Jones Street when you should have taken Smith Lane. Would it help you to feel bad about your mistake? No. Until you turned around and changed directions, you'd never reach your destination. So when you have sinned, come to me and confess. I'll freely forgive you. Then take the important step of repenting by turning your life around. I'll redirect you and steer you toward your holy destination.

Your Loving Father,
>God

== == ==   == == == == == == == == ==

THE FULL ENTRY FEE

With my own eyes I have seen your salvation.

Luke 2:30 NCV

My Child,

>Do you ever look at well-known Christian men and think their faith is in a whole different league from yours? *They are the faithful greats,* you think. *I'm just a small-time Christian.* Listen. I don't grade my saints. I paid the same price to redeem you that I did to redeem the most prominent Christian speaker or theologian in the world. I paid the full kingdom entry fee—the sinless life of my Son.

So stop comparing yourself to others. Let me show you who you are in Christ. Let me show you your own salvation and how I want to use your gifts. Your faith in Jesus is what brought you into my family. You're precious in my sight!

Your Loving Father,
>God

== == ==   == == == == == == == == ==

"WASTING" TIME

**I wait for the LORD, my soul waits,
and in his word I put my hope.**

Psalm 130:5 NIV

My Son,

>Many people equate waiting with wasting time. They see times of inactivity as a total write-off. But I see waiting as the soil of faith in which your life in me can grow sure and strong.

What will you learn when you're willing to wait? You'll learn that you don't have all the answers, and in time you'll find that I do. You'll learn that action, if it's the wrong action, can be worse than no action at all. You'll learn that faith is a dance, a dance in which I must lead. You'll learn to trust my character while you're waiting for my guidance, and you'll learn to lean into my love even when it's silent. So center your spirit on me and hope in my Word as you wait.

The One Worth Waiting For,
>God

== == ==   == == == == == == == == ==

I'M READING YOUR HEART

He has showed you, O man, what is good. And what
does the LORD require of you? To act justly and to
love mercy and to walk humbly with your God.

Micah | 6:8 NIV

My Child,

>I created you to make a difference in the world. Does that mean I
expect you to be elected president or head up a huge corporation or
spearhead a missionary effort? Those things are certainly possible,
but you don't have to achieve big things to please me.

I want you to live your life honestly, without a lot of fanfare. Respect
other people, and treat them fairly. Show mercy and simple kindness
as Jesus did. And walk with me a day at a time. The movers and
shakers of your society may rack up political and financial power, but
I'm not impressed. I'm reading your heart, not your bankbook. Deeds
of quiet humility are what earn interest in my kingdom.

The One Whose Will Is Perfect,
>God

== == ==   == == == == == == == == ==

DON'T BE AFRAID TO SPEAK

You will receive power when the Holy Spirit comes on you; and you will be my witnesses in Jerusalem, and in all Judea and Samaria, and to the ends of the earth.

Acts | 1:8 NIV

Dear Child,

>Do you feel shy and little bit tongue-tied when you speak about your faith? That's not surprising. When faith is genuine, talking about it taps into some pretty powerful emotions. Never be ashamed of your emotions.

Just pray before you speak, and let my Holy Spirit take over. He'll give you his power and his clarity. He'll help you speak with such simple, honest candor that those who hear your words will be moved by what you say. They'll see something in your life that they'll want in their own. So don't worry about having the perfect words. Trust my Spirit, and speak freely.

The Communicator,
>God

== == ==   == == == == == == == == ==

WHAT COMPELS YOU?

Christ's love compels us.

| 2 Corinthians | 5:14 NIV |

Dear Son,

>What compels you to get out of bed in the morning? What
motivates you to do your work? Are you still trying to live up to your
parents' overachievement expectations? Are you trying to be the
most recognized at what you do? Are you trying to be the super-dad
who can do it all—raise perfect children, have the ideal marriage,
and still outperform everyone at work? If so, it's no wonder you fall
into bed at night exhausted.

Go back to square one, my son, and examine your motives. Why are
you jumping through all of these hoops? Invite Jesus to be the motive
behind all you do, and you'll feel your weariness lifting. Listen to his
words: "Come to me . . . and I'll give you rest."

The Love That Compels You,
>God

== == ==   == == == == == == == == ==

THE NEAR AND THE FAR

He came and preached peace to you who were far away and peace to those who were near. For through him we both have access to the Father by one Spirit.

Ephesians | 2:17–18 NIV

Dear Child,

>Jesus is an equal-opportunity Savior. When he came to earth bringing my message of peace, it wasn't just for the super-religious. (In fact, the super-religious frustrated him the most. He saw right through their pious posing to their hidden pride.) Jesus came for everyone. He brought the good news that anyone can have a relationship with me.

Are you near to me today? Do you know you're my child? Or are you far away? Do you feel uncomfortable or unworthy in my presence? The truth is, if it weren't for Jesus, no one could approach me with confidence. But because of him, everyone can. So come to me today from wherever you are—however near or far.

The One Who Waits,
>God

== == ==   == == == == == == == == ==

THE TIGHTROPE AND THE NET

On My arm they will trust.

| Isaiah | 51:5 NKJV |

My Son,

>Does it seem at times that you're walking a tightrope of anxiety over a sea of bad news? Daily headlines reporting world hunger, racial unrest, drugs, violence, international conflict, and a fluctuating economy leave you a little shaky.

I want you to learn to walk confidently. I want you to know that my arms are the rescue net beneath all of life's uncertainty. Whatever situation the world is in, you can trust in my protection and abide in my peace. When you're walking with me, trusting in me, obeying me, you can't fall further than I am able to catch you. So when headlines deliver bad news, focus on this bit of good news. I am with you. And I'm in it for the long haul.

Your Rescue Net,
>God

== == ==   == == == == == == == == ==

MY UNIQUE PERSPECTIVE

Do not be wise in your own eyes;
fear the Lord and shun evil.

Proverbs 3:7 NIV

My Child,

>Are you following your own personal life plan? Have you said things like "I'll marry at this point; I'll have children here; I'll concentrate on my career at this point" and so on? Your plan of action may seem very wise according to your view of things. But it's like the old saying: "You can't see the forest for the trees." You are too close to your own life to have the perspective you need.

I am over you, beside you, and within you, which gives me a unique perspective. What's more, I'm the one who created you, and I know what's best for you. So don't go with your own program. Trust me to show you mine. Then follow it.

The One Who Knows What's Best,
>God

FORMING THEIR FAITH

**These commandments that I give you today are
to be upon your hearts. Impress them on your children.
Talk about them when you sit at home and when you walk
along the road, when you lie down and when you get up.**

Deuteronomy | 6:6–7 NIV

Dear Child,

>What are your kids learning today that they can keep as adults?
What will they be able to hang on to from their formative years? I
hope they'll remember times of love and laughter, seasons of blessing
and struggle, bedtime prayers, evening meals, family celebrations.

But in the midst of it all, may their strongest memory be the faith they
saw in you—your prayers for them, your words of encouragement,
your loving commitment to me. May they see something so real and
vibrant in you that it draws them to me. Every day let them catch you
in the act of loving me. Nothing in this world will matter more when it
comes to the formation of their own faith.

Your Father and Your Friend,
>God

REAPING THE HARVEST

Do not be deceived: God cannot be mocked. A man reaps what he sows. The one who sows to please his sinful nature, from that nature will reap destruction; the one who sows to please the Spirit, from the Spirit will reap eternal life.

Galatians | 6:7-8 NIV

Dear Child,

>You don't have to be raised on a farm to know that if you want to raise corn, you don't plant turnips. Whatever you put into the ground will come out of the ground. That's how it works.

Well, exactly the same principle operates in the spiritual realm. If you plant dishonesty, jealousy, lust, envy, and gossip, the crop you reap will damage and destroy not only you but your loved ones as well. But if you purposely set out to plant love, faith, gentleness, encouragement, and grace, the yield of your life will amaze you. You will harvest an abundant life that lasts forever.

Your Father,
>God

== == ==   == == == == == == == == ==

LIFE'S A FIELD TRIP

I am the Lord your God, who teaches you what is best for you, who directs you in the way you should go.

Isaiah 48:17 NIV

My Child,

>When you were in school, who was your favorite teacher? Was he or she the one who read out of the textbook in a monotone that was so boring you could hardly stay awake? Or did he or she breathe excitement into the lessons by relating them to real life?

The Christian journey is not a boring classroom. It has nothing to do with hiding behind a desk. I am the Teacher who takes you out into the thick of life's real adventures. At every crossroads, I know which turn you should take. At every point of indecision, I know which choice you should make. Begin to see each new day with me as a kind of field trip in which I'll teach you something new as we walk together.

Your Teacher,
>God

== == ==   == == == == == == == == ==

NO SLOPPY IMAGES

I will set before my eyes no vile thing. The deeds of faithless men I hate; they will not cling to me.

Psalm 101:3 NIV

Dear Son,

>Have you ever taken a stroll through a pigpen? If so, you'll never forget it. The odor of the animals clings to you long after you've walked away. The same thing is true of vivid sexual descriptions in books and unsavory scenes in movies or on television. You may think you can simply close the book or flip off the television set and block out the whole experience, but you can't. Those scenes and descriptions actually cling to your spirit as barnyard slop clings to your shoes.

You are, by nature, a spiritually sensitive being. That's the way I created you. But I made you that way so you could absorb my goodness, not so you could absorb the world's filth. Be careful of what you watch, my child.

The Holy One,
>God

== == ==   == == == == == == == == ==

PUT YOUR BOARD IN THE WATER

What good is it, my brothers, if a man claims to have faith but has no deeds? Can such faith save him?

James   2:14 NIV

My Child,

>Suppose someone gives you a top-of-the-line surfboard and a manual on surfing. On day one, you read all about the board itself and how it's made. On day two, you read about the techniques of surfing. On day three, you read about safety in surfing and the history of surfing in the United States. For months you study the manual. You spend hours at the beach watching others on their surfboards. But if you never put your board in the water and feel the thrill of riding a wave, what's the point? You might as well not have a board at all.

The same is true of your faith. You can read and believe everything about me, but if you never put your faith into action, what good is it to either of us? So, how about it? Surf's up!

The Lord of Faith *and* Deeds,
>God

== == ==   == == == == == == == == ==

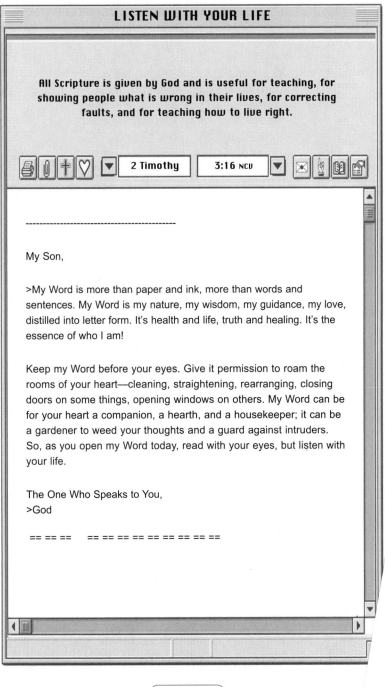

LISTEN WITH YOUR LIFE

All Scripture is given by God and is useful for teaching, for showing people what is wrong in their lives, for correcting faults, and for teaching how to live right.

2 Timothy 3:16 NCV

My Son,

>My Word is more than paper and ink, more than words and sentences. My Word is my nature, my wisdom, my guidance, my love, distilled into letter form. It's health and life, truth and healing. It's the essence of who I am!

Keep my Word before your eyes. Give it permission to roam the rooms of your heart—cleaning, straightening, rearranging, closing doors on some things, opening windows on others. My Word can be for your heart a companion, a hearth, and a housekeeper; it can be a gardener to weed your thoughts and a guard against intruders. So, as you open my Word today, read with your eyes, but listen with your life.

The One Who Speaks to You,
>God

== == ==   == == == == == == == == ==

DIG DOWN DEEP

To all who mourn . . . he will give: beauty
for ashes; joy instead of mourning; praise
instead of heaviness. For God has planted them
like strong and graceful oaks for his own glory.

Isaiah **61:3 TLB**

My Son,

>Animals have learned that in dry seasons there is no moisture near
the surface of the soil, so they dig below the surface to find water that
will quench their thirst. Thirsty trees also send their roots down deep
to reach underground pockets of water.

During your seasons of sorrow, my child, let your roots go down deep
into my love for you. Let my living water satisfy your thirsty spirit.
Though now you may see only the charred ashes of your life, trust
me. I am in the process of renewing you. You can trade those ashes
for beauty, trade your mourning for my joy, and trade your troubled
spirit for my song of praise. Dig down deep, and your healing will
spring forth.

Your Healer,
>God

== == ==   == == == == == == == == ==

BE A RENAISSANCE MAN

They shall rebuild the ancient ruins, repairing cities
long ago destroyed, reviving them though
they have lain there many generations.

Isaiah 61:4 TLB

My Child,

>In your country there are many places where the faith of your
fathers lies in disrepair. The spiritual fire that once burned bright has
grown dim.

I am calling my people to start a renaissance, or rebirth, of
Christianity in your country. I am calling you to be one of those
renaissance men—to stand for truth and to pray for righteousness. I
am calling you to rebuild "the ancient ruins" by fanning the flames of
faith in your own family, church, and city. As you work beside fellow
renaissance Christians, you will see the ruins repaired and the
spiritual devastation turned into revival. Trust me for this rebirth of
faith in your country.

The Rebuilder,
>God

== == ==   == == == == == == == == ==

A LIFETIME OF COMMITMENT

A man will leave his father and mother and be united with his wife, and the two will become one body.

Genesis 2:24 NCV

My Son,

>The culture in which you live is scarred by many broken homes and fractured relationships. Millions of people enter the sacred front door of marriage with a mental back door left open through which they can escape if things don't work out. They have seen so many families fall apart that they are afraid even to have hope in the concept of a lifetime commitment.

But I am calling you to be committed to your marriage covenant. I will give you the strength to remain faithful in the hard times. And when you stick with it, you will experience the lifetime of joy that I've planned for you and your wife. Move with confidence into my call to faithfulness and commitment.

The Lord of Covenant,
>God

== == ==   == == == == == == == == ==

POUR OUT YOUR BEST

Then Mary took a pound of very costly oil of spikenard, anointed the feet of Jesus, and wiped His feet with her hair. And the house was filled with the fragrance of the oil.

John   12:3 NKJV

My Son,

>Mary Magdalene was criticized for wasting a costly jar of oil to anoint the feet of my Son. Her self-righteous critics said she should have sold the oil and spent the money on the poor. But Mary was willing to appear foolish or even wicked in order to pour out her greatest possession for her highest love.

Mary's extravagant love for Jesus contains a powerful lesson for you. In your relationship with my Son, don't hold back. Don't be so practical that you miss the joy of pouring out the best of yourself and your gifts for him and his kingdom. Others may advise caution. But I urge you to throw caution to the wind and love him with all of your heart.

Your Extravagant Father,
>God

HAND ME YOUR CRUTCH

**The . . . lame came to him at the temple;
and he healed them.**

| Matthew | 21:14 KJV |

My Son,

>When you come to me crippled by life, I'm always willing to heal
you. But first you've got to be willing to put down your crutch. Putting
down your crutch will take faith, since you've probably been leaning
on it for quite a while. But how can I teach you to walk if you insist on
clinging to that prop? It will only get in your way.

So what is your crutch? Your education, your addiction, your looks,
your friends, your job, your social standing? It could even be your
religion. Whatever you're leaning on, other than me, has got to go.
Come to me totally powerless, my child. Hand me your crutch, and I'll
have you walking in no time.

Your Healer,
>God

== == ==   == == == == == == == == ==

COLLECT YOUR INHERITANCE

I pray that you will begin to understand how incredibly great his power is to help those who believe him. It is that same mighty power that raised Christ from the dead and seated him in the place of honor at God's right hand in heaven.

Ephesians **1:19–20** TLB

My Child,

>Suppose you received a call from a local attorney telling you to come in and pick up a check for one million dollars left to you by a wealthy relative. How long would it take you to get down to his office?

Well, you have a spiritual inheritance worth far more than a million dollars. It's my incredible power. My power can heal you when you're hurting, guide you when you're lost, and lead you through this challenging adventure called life. It is the same power that raised my Son from the grave—that's how strong it is. Yet at times you mope around like a spiritual pauper with nothing going for you at all. Come to me, my child, and collect your inheritance.

Your Wealthy Relative,
>God

== == ==   == == == == == == == == ==

REFERENCES

Scripture quotations marked NIV are taken from the *Holy Bible, New International Version®* NIV®. Copyright © 1973, 1978, 1984 by International Bible Society. Used by permission of Zondervan Publishing House. All rights reserved.

Verses marked TLB are taken from *The Living Bible,* copyright © 1971. Used by permission of Tyndale House Publishers, Inc., Wheaton, Illinois 60189. All rights reserved.

Scripture quotations marked NCV are taken from *The Holy Bible, New Century Version,* copyright © 1987, 1988, 1991 by Word Publishing, Dallas, Texas 75039. Used by permission.

Scripture quotations marked KJV are taken from the *King James Version* of the Bible.

Scripture quotations marked RSV are taken from *The Revised Standard Version Bible,* copyright © 1952 by the Division of Christian Education of the Churches of Christ in the United States of America and is used by permission.

Scripture quotations marked NKJV are taken from *The New King James Version.* Copyright © 1979, 1980, 1982, Thomas Nelson, Inc.

ABOUT THE AUTHOR

Andy Cloninger, through his many avenues of ministry, meets people where they are and loves them into the truth.

He is currently the contemporary worship leader at Spanish Fort United Methodist Church and plays professionally with acoustic band Dog Named David. He also produces CDs for various bands and leads worship for youth events. Prior to beginning his musical career, Andy and his wife, Jenni, were youth ministers and worked with Young Life Ministries for several years.

Andy, Jenni, and their two children, Kaylee and Drew, make their home in Mobile, Alabama.

If you have enjoyed this book, or if it has
impacted your life, we would like to hear from you.
Please contact us at:

RiverOak Publishing
Department E
P.O. Box 700143
Tulsa, Oklahoma 74170-0143

Additional copies of this book
and other titles in this series
are available from your local bookstore.

E-mail from God for Teens
More E-mail from God for Teens
E-mail from God for Women
E-mail from God for Kids
E-mail from God for Teens screensaver

RIVER
OAK
PUBLISHING